THE

"FLOWER OF GLOSTER"

THE
"FLOWER OF GLOSTER"

by

E. TEMPLE THURSTON

With an introduction by L. T. C. Rolt
and new plates

DAVID & CHARLES   :   NEWTON ABBOT

0 7153 4227 4

A new impression of the book first
published in 1911 by Williams and
Norgate, London

Reprinted 1972

© Introduction and plates
L. T. C. Rolt 1968, 1972

Printed in Great Britain by
The Latimer Press, Whitstable
for David & Charles (Publishers) Limited
Newton Abbot, Devon

In the early years of this century the canals of England were an unknown territory and those few outsiders who travelled over them, Aubertin, Black, Bonthron, Neal and Temple Thurston, wrote of their experiences and the people they encountered as though they were traveller's tales from some far-off and primitive country.

Of these pioneer explorers Temple Thurston alone was a professional author and his book has a polish and an artistry which the others lack. While they fell into the great limbo of forgotten books where they are known only to canal bibliophiles, *The Flower of Gloster* enjoyed a modest and deserved success and was reprinted in a cheap, unillustrated edition. Nevertheless, secondhand copies have today become extremely hard to obtain and the present publishers rightly felt that this minor classic of the canals deserved rescuscitating in this new edition in view of the great resurgence of interest in our waterways.

For the canal enthusiast, the chief interest of the book lies in its description of a journey through the Thames & Severn Canal from west to east. For not only was Temple Thurston one of the last to make this voyage, but he helped his boatman, Eynsham Harry, to leg the boat through Sapperton Tunnel. His book would merit survival solely for its memorable account of this journey, now alas unrepeatable.

Unashamedly romantic and picaresque, *The Flower of Gloster* displays a typical Edwardian attitude towards the English countryside and country people. Nowadays we may find it a little too sweet; in books, as in wine, modern taste is for something drier and more astringent. We expect more facts and less philosophising. Yet the book should not be lightly dismissed on this account. As a whole it does convey a memorable picture of a rural England which, despite the coming of canals and railways, had remained at heart unchanged for centuries but was to vanish utterly away under the impact of two world wars and the motor-car invasion. At that time, when country life was hard but placid and uneventful, memories were long. I like particularly the story told by the old man in the Bricklayers Arms at Daneway of how his grandfather met George IV walking down the towpath.

There seems to be a long-standing convention among publishers that any discursive 'country book' of this type must be illustrated by an artist and not by photographs. Back in 1944 I had selected a set of photographs with which to illustrate my own book about another canal journey, *Narrow Boat*, but the publishers made it a condition of acceptance that the book should be illustrated by an artist, who proceeded to use the photographs as his models. What was true in 1944 was also true of *The Flower of Gloster* in 1911 and I think it a pity. However able the illustrator may be, the reader naturally suspects him of artistic licence, of romanticising his subjects. Of course it didn't really look like that', we say, and a lot of this sceptisism, quite unjustly, gets brushed off on to the accompanying text. But for this unfortunate convention, books of this *genre* would supply us with a much more complete and trustworthy record of what England was like before the invasion of technology in the shape of the 'wirescape', the motor road, the television and all the other concomit-ants of an urban civilisation bursting at the seams, trying to get the best out of town and country and ruining both in the process.

In this case it has been possible to do belated justice to the author's veracity. For Mrs Temple Thurston most kindly lent to me an album of photographs which her late husband took on his canal voyage and has courteously permitted the publishers to use some of the best of them to illustrate this edition in place of W. R. Dakin's colour plates which, to be honest, are no loss. In these photographs the cool, objective eye of the author's camera has recorded for all time that such characters as Mrs Izod, the sun-bonneted old ferrywoman at Fladbury Mill, or 'Old Willum', the lengthman on the Thames & Severn, waiting expectantly for the boats that never came, were real people uncoloured by the romantic imaginations of Edwardian author or illustrator. They are characters closer in spirit to medieval England than to our fretful age. Like Alfred Williams, the Swindon smith who recorded so percipiently the life of the Wiltshire villages in his *Villages of the White Horse* (Duckworth, 1913), we should be grateful to Temple Thurston for recording an immemorial way of life on the eve of its dissolution.

Paradoxically, vestiges of that life survived most stubbornly on the canals, one of the earliest agents of revolutionary change. For the boats and the boatmen that Temple Thurston recorded in words and photographs remind me of those which I encountered between thirty and forty years after. Eynsham Harry is no stranger to me. I have known several boaters on the Oxford canal who might have played his part to the life. But now they are gone also.

THE "FLOWER OF GLOSTER"

Temple Thurston's photographs betray the provenance of many of W. R. Dakin's drawings in the text, most notably that of the *Flower of Gloster* locking through at Cropedy on the Oxford Canal. Which is Eynsham Harry? The album supplies no answer to the riddle, but I suspect that the respectable figure in shirt sleeves was the lock keeper and that Eynsham Harry is the character on the towpath facing the camera held by 'that writer-chap from Lunnon'. He has his memorial here in the graphic word-picture that the writer-chap painted of him.

L. T. C. Rolt

TO

BELLWATTLE

LONDON,
August 1911.

MY DEAR BELLWATTLE,

A wedding present is always inadequate. I have no doubt if I gave you a dog, you would be best pleased with that ; but you have Dandy, and lavish such affection on him as makes me at times regard him in the light of a thief; I have thought of other things besides dogs, and am reduced at last to offering you this—this chronicle of the journey of the *Flower of Gloster*. If ever it takes you—only for one hour—away from the need of forgetfulness to the joy of remembrance, then in some sense this little wedding present will not be so inadequate as it may seem.

Your CRUIKSHANK.

P.S.—Thirteen copies count as twelve. This will well-nigh lead you into the higher mathematics when you come to calculate your royalties.

CONTENTS

LIST OF PLATES

THE
"FLOWER OF GLOSTER"

I

THE DISCOVERER

I HAVE ever believed that the world is a place to wander in. Indeed, if Time be made for slaves, then Space is made for free-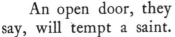men. It is only the freeman who, one bright morning, when the long brown buds like cornu-copias are bursting on the beech tree, can sling a knapsack across his shoulders, drop the key of the house in the deepest corner of his pocket, and set out down the road of discovery.

An open door, they say, will tempt a saint.
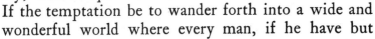
If the temptation be to wander forth into a wide and wonderful world where every man, if he have but

the heart for it, may be his own discoverer, then I can well believe the truth of all they say.   Now, of open doors there may be many, and of saints who yield to their temptation, no less.   But the heart for the spirit of discovery, that is a different business altogether.   You will as like find it in a sinner as a saint.   There are few, indeed, who have it now.

For this, I would urge you, is the spirit of discovery ; not merely that setting of one's prow towards the far horizon of the unknown—that is the spirit of adventure.   The spirit of discovery lies in the eye and in the mind.   He whose sight is young enough to find anew the world that has been found by others, he is the discoverer and, by right of that power of which he holds the secret, a man may reveal new worlds wherever he goes.

There is none too much of that spirit left in any of us now.   Guide-books and the like have taken all the freshness out of our point of view.   A man travels to see what others have seen before him ; he buys his beauties of the road at second hand.   They go so far as to give him reduction for a quantity. Cheap tours comprising the greatest number of sights in the shortest space of time are innovations our Grandfathers would have shuddered at.   They read books of travel in those days.   But your guide is no traveller.   He knows his beauties off by heart as the verger knows the little history of his church. So well does he know them, moreover, that they are no longer beauties for him, but only catch-words set to trap the tourist's ear.

"This Tower," says he, with a ready eye to mark his listener's face, "was built in the year of our Lord——" And when he says "the year of our Lord," he means to astonish you then.

I remember the showman in the Whispering Gallery of St Paul's. As I entered by the narrow doorway into that vast space beneath the dome, a tiny little man in a black gown took me in hand at once, at once began pouring forth his monotonous doggerel of facts—figures of height and breadth and depth. The Lord himself knows what they were, for I have long forgotten them.

"Now go," said he, "round to the other side, and I'll whisper to you."

In the hands of such men as these, somehow or other, one is numbed into obedience. Meekly I went. Then, as he leant his head against the wall, there came from the lips of this insignificant little creature a voice which, in one great volume of sound, shook me and made me tremble as it thundered by.

"Can you hear what I'm saying?" shouted the voice.

When I replied that I could, he nodded his head to me across the mighty gulf and smiled as one who well approves of himself. Had he been Sir Christopher himself, he could not have looked more pleased.

For a few moments, then, I sat there opposite the

door looking down alone into the chasm of the nave. But only for a few moments was I allowed to marvel at the wonder of it all ; only for a few moments was I allowed to discover it for myself. At the very commencement of my meditations, there entered two more visitors through the door, and the little man began again his miserable rigmarole of heights and breadths and depths.

I bethought me then of an excellent thing to do, and, leaning my head against the wall, I whispered in the sweetest voice I knew :

" For God's sake stop that silly nonsense ! "

For the brief space of time in which my voice must take to travel round, I looked across and waited. A second later I saw him stagger, and the visitors, frightened, looked about them as the thunder of my words resounded in their ears.

A whispering gallery, you may perceive, has its advantages ; but a guide, so far as I have ever been able to discover, has none.   He would willingly ruin every illusion you might have.

" Around that corner," says he, " you will come face to face with St Mark's and the four bronze horses—— "

But for Heaven's sake, say I, let me turn the corner for myself.   What else was a corner made for but to hide at once the beauties it reveals !

Yet that is never the spirit of the guide, for the guide-book is his litany.

"I'll go," said I one day, "where are no guides and scarce a map is printed. Who knows his way about the canals of England?"

"They begin at Regent's Park," said a man.

"And then?" I asked him.

"There's one passes near Slough on the Great Western. I've seen it from the train."

"If that's all that's known about them," said I, "I'll get a barge myself and go on till I stop."

II

THE " FLOWER OF GLOSTER "

THESE things are easily said. It is the devil and all to accomplish them. Everyone I knew, I asked, " Where can I get a barge ? "

It was a foolish question to make, and one to which, as often as not, I received the foolish reply, " What for ? "

What in the name of Heaven could one want a barge for, unless it were in which to travel on those waters where all barges may be found ? Out of its element, doubtless, it is the ugliest thing the hand of man ever created ; but sinking low in the still waters of those silent canals, its blunt, good-natured nose thrusting the long ripples to either side, travelling from one old town to another with its happy-go-lucky two and three miles an hour, it is the most wonderful vehicle in the world.

There came a time when I grew sick of that answer. Then I went down to the Regent's Park Basin, where all those barges going east, west, and north, collect and discharge their cargo.

"Hire a barge?" said they. "Where do you want to go?"

"Anywhere," I replied. "You don't think I'm looking for an express method of conveyance."

They gazed from one to the other with amusement that was more or less respectful. The world is full of fools, of course, and none so great a fool is there as he who would think to find time for play with that which is another man's labour. They did not say as much as this. They thought it in their several ways, every single one of them. I doubt if I should have shown as much respect to the man who came and asked me where he could get pens, ink, and paper, for that he was going to spend his holidays a-writing.

But the bargee, notwithstanding all that reputation he has earned, has the innate sense of politeness which only the breeding of nature can give to a man. More than half his days, gliding peacefully through those winding stretches of water, with the great breadth of a glorious country on either side of him, he is in closest touch with the best that nature has to give. Often without education, without even the knowledge of how to read or write, he lives a life of complete and untouched simplicity. He is a law almost to himself.

Now they would have you believe, the apostles of civilisation, that man is a social creature, thriving, developing, progressing through the medium of the

community.   That elusive word—gentleman—which
no one understands and few can emulate, has been
coined by a class calling itself Society.   Society has
bred the gentleman, just as the Irish have bred the
race-horse, the only difference being that the Irish-
man knows a race-horse when he sees it.

But just as the race-horse is not the only animal
of that species in existence, so the gentleman is not
the only man.   What is more, he is not the only
gentleman.   The fact of the matter is, Society has
lost its cunning in breeding the race.   They have
outbred the stock which made them famous.   Nature
can breed far finer gentlemen now than ever Society
puts forth into the field.   For it is not luxury
which is the food for the species, but that work
and that labour bringing the sweat honestly to the
brow.   And the bargee, for all his rough-and-readi-
ness, is one of the many gentlemen of Nature I
have met.

When, failing to discover at the Regent's Park
Basin where I might hire a barge, I betook myself
to headquarters and made inquiries at the offices of
one of the canal navigations, I was told that I
probably did not realise the class of men with whom
I should have to mix.

"They're not gentlemen, you know," said the
officer with a smile.   "And if you take out a barge
yourself, you'll probably come a great deal in contact
with them."

" Now what," said I, " do you mean by a gentleman ? "

I think his smile was compassionate. For the moment he believed I was as ignorant of the matter as himself. Whereupon he shrugged his shoulders as one who would say : " My dear sir—a gentleman ? To a gentleman the term explains itself."

But it was his shrug of the shoulders that I answered. What is more, I took the opportunity of translating it as I chose.

" You see," said I, " how unhappy a word that is. A shrug of the shoulders won't dispose of it. Nevertheless, in your opinion it comes to this—the bargee is not a gentleman. But if neither you nor I know what a gentleman is—for I swear to God that I don't,—why should it concern you that I hire a barge, or me that I must mix with bargees in the hiring of it ? "

Now the offices of the canal navigation are dusty rooms. The dust hangs heavily on all the maps that surround the walls. Were it the office of a mortuary or the room of the little man who kept the records in the Morgue, there would be more business done there in an idle day. As it is, so far as I could see, the only company the officer keeps are his papers. To be suddenly confronted, then, by a strange individual, who immediately plunges into some abstruse controversy as to the meaning of the word gentleman, was a little more than he could bear. I think some of the dust of the office must long have got into his brain, for the more I said, the more confused he grew. Had I brought a feather brush with me and ruthlessly swept the dust from every shelf and cranny in the place, I could scarce have upset him more.

When, then, I saw him growing red in the face, I changed the subject.

"In any case," said I, "it concerns me more to know if I can hire a barge."

"You can hire twenty," he replied. "But I prefer you did it than I. Do you intend to sleep on board?"

I confessed it had been my intention.

"Then you won't want an old manure barge?"

"I might feel a prejudice against that," said I.

He fell to looking over some papers. Presently he raised his head.

"There's a barge at Oxford," he informed me. "She used to be on the Thames and Severn Canal— carried stone—wood sometimes. She's just been done up at Braunston and brought along there. If you went down there at once and saw the owner, he might hire her to you for a couple of months, and make a bit out of it himself."

"What's her name?" said I.

"The *Flower of Gloster*."

Now when he said that, then I knew she was mine. The *Flower of Gloster*! The name alone would have disinfected her of all the disagreeable odours in the world.

III

THE " FLOWER OF GLOSTER "

continued

In matters of this kind, a fine sounding name has much to do with the success of the venture. Alice Louise may have been at heart a noble creature, meaning all that was admirable in a wife to the man who named his barge after her. But to you who know nothing of Alice Louise and all her sterling qualities, there is not that sweetness in the name which will destroy a cargo of gas-water of all its unpleasant odours.

If the clothes he wears, and the title he has won, have anything to do with your respect of a man, then look to the painting and the naming of your barge. And if she have half so fine a name as the *Flower of Gloster*, take her at once as I did. A coat of paint is, any day, an easier matter than a christening.

For Fate orders these things much to her own liking. All the ships that ever made history for England were nobly called. The *Bellerophon* ! There was a boastful name, well chosen to carry into banishment the greatest maker of history the world has ever seen. Fate looked to it, too, that he was greatly named as well. What but great things could come

to pass on the *Victory*? Where better could they happen than at Trafalgar!

With such a name as Nelson, battles at sea were made to be won; though, indeed, I knew a bank clerk of that surname who never so much as won the approbation of his manager. True, they had not christened him Horatio, and doubtless that made much of the difference.

"But all this," said I, as the officer regarded my sudden decision with amazement, "all this is a matter of sentiment and comes nowhere in our reckoning."

"'Twould be more to the point," replied he, "if you inquire the cost of the hiring."

"At any price," said I, "the *Flower of Gloster* would be cheap."

Whereupon he settled back in his chair, together with the dust that I had raised upon my entrance, and, thanking him, as any man should be thanked for coming so far out of his groove as to speak to me, I left him and set off for Oxford.

IV

OXFORD

" Down in the town, off the bridges and the grass
They are sweeping up the leaves to let the people pass,
Sweeping up the old leaves, golden-reds and browns,
Whilst the men go to lecture with the wind in their gowns."

FRANCES CORNFORD wrote that of Cambridge—of an
autumn morning, too. It kept singing in my head,
nevertheless, as I walked
through Oxford that
morning in May to find
my *Flower of Gloster.*

If a stanza be true
in autumn, it is true in
all the seasons beside. It
mattered little whether
it were Oxford or Cam-
bridge to me. That the
leaves were young and
golden, just topping the
old walls of the college gardens, giving you pictures
framed preciously through the narrow doorways of

the college gates ; that it would be whole months of
spring and summer before they fell again and raced
with the gusty winds of autumn down the streets,
made no difference to the simple truth of that little
rhyme.   The men *were* going to lecture, and the
wind *was* in their gowns.   So I lilted the lines to myself as I found my way down to the canal side.

" I ran out to the apple tree and plucked an apple down,
    And all the bells were ringing in the old grey Town."

" 'Tis the old grey Town that matters," said I.
" We shall have the apples fast enough."

I don't care how dull or dusty may be the minds
of the dons and pedagogues who live within the
walls of Oxford now.   It is the old grey Town that
matters and the few customs that remain.

One New Year's eve I was taken to the college
of Magdalen to hear the carols sung.   In a great hall
with massive ceiling and with panelled walls we
were given mulled claret to drink, from Elizabethan
silver jugs ; plates of mince-pies were handed round ;
all the old customs were observed to the last letter.
At some short time before midnight every illumination was extinguished.   Then by the light of a
great fire burning brightly in the open grate, with
the reflection of its flames dancing on the polished oak,
winking from the silver jugs upon the long refectory
tables, the choir began its singing of the old-time
English carols.   But it is not that which I remember

The Flower of Gloster locking through at Cropredy, Oxford Canal

Boaters encountered on the Oxford Canal

best of all. As the hour of midnight struck and the
New Year was on the very threshold of the world,
they flung wide open the great windows and, through
the old grey Town, we heard the pealing of a hundred
bells. It was as if each one of them with ringing
voice were crying out, "The Old Year is dead—
long live the New ! "

But for their buildings and their customs, all
Oxford might be dead. Even now it is a city of
dust and shadows. The masters of learning who sit
in the deep-welled seats of their college windows,
gazing across the grave, green gardens, are no more
than the myriad particles of decay which slowly have
been settling there upon the mullions for the last few
hundred years.

"When a man has had no Alma Mater other
than the light of day and such odd jests of chance as
circumstance has chosen to shield him with, then,"
thought I, "this is just the sort of thing he will be
bound to say of the universities."

It is of more concern to everyone that I found
my barge. But before that be come to, I must say
some word of the offices of the Oxford and Birmingham Canal Navigation. How long they have been
employed to that purpose, I do not know. In comparison with the age of the building it cannot have
been for many years. It is built of that grey stone
from which all the colleges have been erected, and,
by now, the yellow growth of age has toned it to

" By a narrow wooden door . . . you are given sudden entrance. "

wonderful shades which bring colour both to your imagination and your eye.

By a narrow wooden door in a high stone wall you are give sudden entrance to a garden bright with colour, warm with the scent of flowers. There, in spring, the violet aubrietia blends its masses with the faint blue of the periwinkle ; the double arabis spreads its carpet of snow before the purple iris and the scarlet tulip buds.

In the midst of those drab surroundings where lies the canal quite close to the railway station, this unexpected oasis of colour, hidden beyond high walls which keep it from the eyes of passers-by, is like a jewel set in lead. It was by chance I visited it—the same chance which has ever been my Alma Mater.

And on to this garden look the high windows of the canal company's offices. When I came there a shower of rain had just been falling and a thousand glittering diamond drops of water were hanging from the points of the leaves on the lilac trees. The air was cool, and the whole place was fresh with the light of a bright blue sky of spring.

"Were I the canal company's officer in Oxford," said I to the manager in charge, "this should be my pension."

"I call it part of my salary, myself," said he. "Come out and see a new sort of sweet-scented stock I've got. One plant will scent a whole room."

We went out to a little glass-house where he

forces his young shoots and keeps the prize speci-
mens of his horticulture.   A tortoise was in somnolent
charge of the whole establishment.   If Bellwattle were
here, thought I, how she would surprise the canal
company's officer with an address to the tortoise !
There was an animal who would have looked
after her interests and God's as well without so
much as making a fuss over the serving of two
masters !

With an animated expression in his face, he
expatiated to me upon one plant after another.   I
forget what he called this ; I forget what he called
that.   They were all beautiful and they all had Latin
names.   When chance is your Alma Mater, you
must pretend a knowledge of the dead languages and
get along through this life as best you can.

" Indeed ! " said I—and " Yes ! " said I to every
name he gave.

Ignorance is a luxury only to be afforded by the
very, very wise.

Could I but quote Latin, doubtless there would be
much respect for me.   But that I don't, probably
loses me no more.   There are always those who do
not understand, and to put a man at that disadvantage
when you have him in conversation is a risking of all
his approval.

I only thought well of my canal official's knowledge because I contrived to deceive him that I knew
as much myself.   Had I known that he was aware

of my ignorance, I should have disliked him very much indeed.

" What's your busiest time of the year here ? " I asked him, when he had filled my head with names.

" Spring," he replied.

I looked at the rows of boxes with their young shoots neatly thinned.

" I suppose it must be," said I.

V

OXFORD—*continued*

BUT they know such a deuce of a lot in Oxford. They are too clever for me by half.

Into a curio shop, calling itself Lares & Penates, I walked—as is my weakness wherever a curio shop is to be found,—and there bought some little thing that had the taste of age about it. It was not that antiquity of which they make a special study in Birmingham, despatching to the old houses in the old towns of England where they will tell you it has been in the family for generations. Its age, at least, was genuine. Not that I know—but I say so.

"Send it round," said I, "to the inn where I am staying. I'll pay on delivery."

And round it came in the care of a young man of twenty, who deposited it on my table and smiled. It was a warm day and, taking out his handkerchief, he wiped the perspiration from his brow.

"That will be another sixpence," said I to myself. It was as plain as writing it on the bill.

"And to whom do I make out the cheque?" I asked.

" Lairs and Penaits," said he.

I looked up with my pen raised.

" Lairs and Penaits," he repeated.

" Will they understand that at the bank ? " I
inquired. For, mind you, I had not then seen their
name above the door.

" Oh yes—Lairs and Penaits—they'll understand
it all right. It means 'ouseold gods."

Then I remembered. Latin syntax ! It made
me feel quite young again.

> " Common are to either sex,
> Artifex and opifex."

A doggerel rhyme of words which play some
nasty tricks with your Latin exercise whenever you
are fool enough to use them.

" You must forgive my asking," said I.

" Oh well—it ain't everybody as knows," he
replied. " Not even in Oxford. It's only when
you're heducated, of course."

I took my place without a word.

" I don't say that meaning nothin'," he continued. Perhaps he saw the look of humility on
my face, and was thinking of his sixpence. No
man will pay for the virtue of humility. It is not
cheap at any price. Certainly it is not so cheap
as it feels. Wherefore, hastening to reassure
me, he added : " I only came across it myself
by chanst."

" How's that ? " said I.

" Well," he replied, " when I'm not doing messages for them, I do a bit of window-cleanin'.

I saw it in a book. I was cleanin' the windows of a school. It was lyin' on a desk. Now I'm always sharp on them things. I'd sooner read a book like that than any novel. Lairs and Penaits—I saw it there in the book."

" But which means household gods ? " said I—" Lairs or Penaits ? "

" Well, both of them. Only, one's old Roman Latin, and the other's Italian Latin."

I looked at him with envy.

" I wish I was educated like you," said I.

" Well, you can't 'elp it 'ere in Oxford," said he. " I say it's the air of the place—it makes you want to know things like that."

" And such a help to window-cleaning," said I.

He glanced at me quickly.

" Ye—es," said he—but oh ! so very slowly ! It might have been a word of two syllables.

VI

JOSEPH PHIPKIN—OWNER

Down by the canal wharf, I found the *Flower of Gloster*. What with her new paint, the thought too, no doubt, that soon she would be mine, I could have picked her out from a thousand others. Their ideas of colour are very southern, these people of the barges. Much is to be found of the gypsy in their habits, their appearance, and their minds. Indeed, they are no less than water gypsies, having that same barbaric, Latin eye for colour with the painting of their boats as the country gypsy has for the decoration of his caravan.

The exterior of the cabin in the aft part of the boat is gaily painted with vivid reds, glaring yellows, greens, and black. Water-cans, buckets, the shallow pails for the horse's provender, even the horse's traces too—a set of wooden beads strung loose upon a cord—all are painted with their Spanish joy of colour. And this is not the closest relation of their minds to that country which has fed the world with gypsies. I puzzled for a long while before I realised

that the scenes which are painted on the panels on
their cabin exteriors are rough pictures of those
castles, not which you build, but which you find in
Spain. What is more, these people are lovers of
brass—a sure sign of the gypsy. Inside many a

cabin of the boats which ply their long journeys and
are the only homes of those who work them, you
will find the old brass candlesticks, brass pots and
pans, all brilliantly polished, glittering in the light.
A brass lamp hangs from the bulkhead. It does not
swing, for the motion of these barges is like to no
other vehicle in which I have ever ridden. It is no
motion, or it is motion asleep.

It was when I had put myself in the way of a bargain with Joseph Phipkin, owner of the *Flower of Gloster*, that I ventured to lead the conversation back to where my thoughts of gypsies were still waiting.

There is no frame of mind so conducive to an amicable interchange of ideas as when two men have settled a matter of purchase to their liking. Both are warm with the virtue of having given, both secretly with joy in that they have received. Had it left but a shirt to my back for the journey, I should not have grudged Mr Phipkin the price he had asked for the *Flower of Gloster*. And had I broken her nose against the first bridge I met, then, thinking of the price he had received, doubtless he would have been philosophical. There was no such thing as a treaty between us. The money left my pocket with that ease and familiarity with which money always treats me. Judging by the way his fingers closed upon it, it found its way into his purse in much the same manner. There are men who spend money in this world; there are men who receive it; and the two are always coming together over the question of a bargain. Business would be a more ugly affair than it is if such were not the case.

" And, now that's settled," said I, " where am I to look for a man ? I want a man and a horse."

" Are yer particular ? " he asked.

" Needs must," said I ; " not only to the devil's driving."

He let that pass, still waiting for my answer.

"I shall get more to the manner of the thing," thought I, "as I go along. The sooner I am outside Oxford, the better." The fact of the matter was, that window-cleaner had upset all my balance of men and things.

"I'm particular," I went on, "that he's kind to his beast. Nothing else worries me."

"Well, sir, they're all that," said he, "a man don't quarrel with his bread and butter, 'less it ain't cut to his liking."

"I'd sooner have your observation," said I, "than half the learning in Oxford." And that being the kind of remark one makes to a man when one is in a good humour with the world in general, he took every syllable of it to swell himself with pride.

"'Tain't no good," said he seriously, "going about this world with yer eyes shut. What I say is, if a man has to be thrown amongst men it's no waste of time if he tries to understand 'em."

"It's a policy," said I, "that applies not only to men."

"I'd do the same with wild beasts," he replied.

"And even there," said I, "it might be to your advantage."

"I can well believe it," he returned seriously, for I had but to say a thing with a straight face and he took me promptly at my word. "But about this man," he continued. "What yer want is some decent fellar with a horse, what'll look after yer goin' through the locks. That's how I take it."

I complimented him on the gift he had of a ready understanding.

" Well," said he, " I've no time to waste puzzlin' out what people mean. If my understandin' ain't good enough to take their meanin' first go-off, it's no good my doin' business with 'em. Now the man yer want is Eynsham Harry. He's not working just now—won't be for more than a month. But he knows the canals blindfold—been a-boatin' all his life. Born on a barge—he'll die on a barge, too. He's a dark-lookin' fellar ; but you'll find all these people are dark—dark hair, dark eyes, that browny sort of skin, winter and summer. It ain't the sun."

Now, this was just the point for which I had been waiting ; for whatever may be written of places, their greater interest is the people who inhabit them. So you make a home, by those who dwell in it. When, then, he spoke of their complexion, I let him go no further.

" Has the bargee any definite origin ? " I inquired. " Does any one know where he comes from ? "

He shook his head. He shook it wisely, as though much were to be said upon a matter to which as yet he had not given the fulness of his attention.

" They're not like ordinary people, anyhow," said he—" I've studied them here and there, and I've noticed that. They're all dark—a brown-eyed lot, I call 'em. Yer see, they never 'malgamate. They fruitify amongst themselves."

" Of course, if they do that——" said I.

" Well, that's the way I understand it," he replied.

Now, I would not have disturbed his understanding for the world, and, so far as it confirmed my ideas about the water gypsy, I was constrained to be satisfied. Undoubtedly they are of Southern extraction. Their dark, black hair, their olive skin, that soft expression of lethargy in the eyes, all point to the blood of some race other than the fair-haired Saxon. Perhaps vagabondage is in the blood and these are the outward and visible signs of a grace that I for one would not be sorry to count amongst my virtues, always supposing I were able to talk in the plural about such matters.

There was one thing more, however, upon which I needed enlightenment. The name of the man he had recommended had a touch of the uncommon about it. I asked him if it were a nickname.

" Not exactly," he replied. " The men are named here by the places they hail from. What his real name is, I don't know. He's probably forgotten it himself by this time. Harry's his name, and he comes from Eynsham."

" And where shall we find him ? " said I.

With a throw of his head in its direction, Mr

Phipkin indicated a public-house called the Nag's Head.

"If yer ever want a bargee in Oxford," said he, "look for him there."

And without doubt this was the soundest piece of information Mr Phipkin had yet given me.

VII

THE BARGAIN
—OXFORD

OVER an affair of this nature, when the question of
payment is invariably left to so much of a sense of
honour as you care to lay claim to, it is as well to
open the proceedings as far from the matter in hand
as possible.

In reply to my suggestion, the landlord brought
in whisky and water to the little parlour of the Nag's
Head, where I have no doubt private transactions
have taken place ever since the canals were opened.
It is an old inn. The floors are strewn with sawdust.
The benches are well-worn and polished. Through
the door from the bar comes the sound of thick

Mrs Izod, the Ferrywoman at Fladbury Mill, River Avon

A Severn Trow lying at Stonehouse Basin, Stroudwater Navigation

laughter, heavy voices, and the brittle clink of glasses. One glance within reminded me of the drinking-houses along the quay-side in Marseilles. In a shadow three men were playing cards with a pack whose nearly every feature had been defaced by the grimy hands through which they had passed. In the corners, men stood in groups and talked. Every man talked. No man listened. But this always happens where men are gathered together for the sole purpose of drinking.

In our little parlour it was just the reverse. Each one of us wanted to listen while the other talked, for a man scents business no less readily than he does danger. A certain flavour of it is set free from the situation; and, have you but the slightest sensitiveness to such things, you must get wind of it at once. When, therefore, such a case arises, it is wise to say as little as possible.

Now of all the men I have ever met who were keen to the susceptibility of such a moment, Eynsham Harry was the most acute. With a slow but steady eye upon Mr Phipkin, he listened attentively while that gentleman portentously explained the meaning of my presence in the parlour of the Nag's Head.

" Harry," said he, " this gentleman has taken the *Flower of Gloster* for a month. He's goin' to do a trip over the canals."

Eynsham Harry nodded his head in silence, and for a moment his eyes met mine, though they quickly fell

again as though, under the circumstances, I might be
sensitive to his scrutiny.

"I'm on some fool's errand," thought I, "and
the man is sorry for me. But in this world such
things may easily happen without one being sorry for
oneself."   His glance in no way disconcerted me, and,
after it, we drank our whisky for a moment without
speaking.   Had it been a meeting of the council of
ten, we could scarcely have been more serious over it.

Presently Mr Phipkin broke in again.

"This gentleman wants a man and a horse,
Harry," said he — "do you think we could
find 'em ? "

The point of the matter was now coming home
to him. I wanted a man and a horse. Obviously
he was the man. He had a horse as well, and for
the next month was doing nothing ; whereupon he
became more cautious than ever.

"I've no doubt," he replied at length. "Does
the gentleman want to find 'en in Oxford ? "

"I want to start away to-day," said I.

He shifted his cap and scratched his head.

"How about Jack Leamington ? " asked Mr
Phipkin, and, under cover of his glass, he dropped a
wink to me

"Jack's all right," Eynsham Harry replied ; "but
I don't know what the gentleman wants to pay."

"A pound a week," said I ; "I'll find the man's
food—the horse's too."

Mr Phipkin looked at him as one who would say, " Now's yer chance ! " But in the light of things as I see them now, this was only a stage in the business which, for myself, I would gladly have completed long ago. But I find they like these methods. It is the one thing British about them. If a deal is to be made, there is always joy in the heart of them over the odd penny that remaineth. That glance of Mr Phipkin's was merely to assure me that he was acting wholly and entirely in my interests. Eynsham Harry took no notice of it.

" Jack Leamington," said he, " would want nearer two."

" Well, " I asked, " supposing you were able to come, what would you want ? "

He looked surprised. You would never have supposed it could have entered his head that I might suggest such a thing.

" Well, sur," said he, " I should leave that to you." And by the tone in his voice it was understood that not only was I a man of honour, but of no little generosity beside.

Now by this I had had enough of bargaining and, when you get into that frame of mind, it goes hard with you if you don't get what you want. For, I take it, in a bargain, one man at least desires to effect an exchange ; and the other, if he cares little what happens, is in far the better position of the two.

" I'll give you thirty shillings," said I, and,

swallowing the rest of my whisky, I put down the glass with a rap upon the trestle table.

For yet another moment he was silent, as though a thousand calculations were passing through his mind. But when I made a movement to be off, preparatory to shaking the sawdust of the place from off my feet, he clinched with me at once.

"I'll take it on," said he, "for a month."

That is the best of leaving these things to men of honour. They are always fools. One pound a week would have paid him handsomely. I notice, however, that there is no such thing as discount on the price of experience. Another time I shall know better.

VIII

THE BEGINNING OF THE JOURNEY

WHEN once your provisions are aboard, your passes signed and paid for, there remains nothing but to hitch your horse to the tow-rope and be off. Here, on the canals, there is no tide to hinder any man. At such an hour you start, because at such an hour before nightfall, when all the locks are closed, you need to be in such and such a place. Indeed, it is the life of a gypsy. Your home you carry with you wheresoever you go, moreover there is not one upon the road who may lift his hand to stay you.

At a quarter past four that afternoon in May, I sat in the stern of the *Flower of Gloster* and watched the tow-line tauten, saw the water-drops shake from off the sodden rope that glistened like a twisted thread of silver in the sunlight, and felt that first faint movement of the barge as she swung round into her gentle, gliding pace.

I pushed the tiller over hard a-starboard, and out went her nose into the canal's centre. One by one the ripples gathered and lengthened on the water, and soon we were leaving the towers and roofs of the old grey town behind us.

Some twenty yards ahead upon the path walked Eynsham Harry with his horse, the tow-line sagging and tautening, sagging and tautening, as she strained or lingered on her way.

Once I lifted my head and looked above me. The sky was just beginning to tinge with primrose.

"Now, were I in London," said I, "my ears would be filled with the shrieks of a thousand motor horns and I could scarcely see the sky for the housetops. What is more, I'm going into a new world where never a soul will trouble to tell me the way."

And then, as though to make the silence more absolute and complete, a peewit rose and swept in

circles round the meadows. " Pee-
wit ! " she cried ; " pee-wit ! "

"It is little sounds," thought I,
" that fill the silences."

For silence is a vessel that may be
filled, or may be broken.   Now in
London we have nothing save the
shattered fragments, which not even the long sleep
of a winter's night can mend.   But in the country,
the song of a lark will fill the pitcher to the brim.
Add but the notes of a thrush, and I have known
it running over.

IX

JOHN AIKIN AND ANNA LÆTITIA

THE first canal to be opened in England was that in 1761, called after the Duke of Bridgewater. Since then, over 14,000 miles of navigable waterways have been brought into service in England and Wales, and scarce a soul is there, but those who work upon them, to know anything of these broad and often beautiful roads—great highways into the heart of the most glorious country in the world.

" 'Tis obvious," said I, when I had read this paragraph again, " that an Englishman has written here. But if his country be not the most beautiful in the world to him, then it goes hard with a man to find beauty anywhere."

Those peasants in the wild mountain villages of Switzerland would doubtless find too much of Nature's gentleness in the long, low stretches of open country that lie across our land. But if Nature has been gentle with you, then gentleness is her greatest beauty in your eyes. For myself, I know I would sooner have the sweep of the open meadows, the

tinkling music of the running streams and the song
of a soaring lark, than all the grandest range of
mountains in Europe.   But then I am not a Swiss,
and Nature herself has looked to it in the selection of
my parents that I should appreciate what she has
seen fit to give me.

Let that be as it may, I would not for a kingdom
have missed those few weeks in the heart of England,
far distant from any of those main thoroughfares
where the dust of motors powders the face of Nature
till she is worse than some painted thing.   Scarce a
soul is to be met along those winding tow-paths, for
you may be sure that where a canal runs from one
town to another, that is the longest way it is possible
to go.   Why, between Banbury and Napton Bottom
there stands the little village of Wormleighton—a
crown of old red houses upon the crest of a high
green hill,—which thrice and again you circle round
before you make one mile upon your journey.   Now
this is not the road a man would take from choice,
and miles you may go, winding and ever winding
through the sleepy level of the meadows, with never a
human being to bid you good-night or good-morrow.

Such are the canals of England to-day.   They
will lead you through the quietest villages, the most
remote of hamlets, with which, to know all the
thousand little clusterings of people, a man might
well spend his lifetime and learn but half of the
country in which he lived.   Indeed, men of research

and patience have devoted their years to its knowledge, and at the end of threescore years and ten have
offered to the press a scarce exhaustive study of just
the county in which they were born.   Such is good

work for one man to do in a lifetime.   And through
these countless places, hidden in the nooks and
crannies of England, the *Flower of Gloster* bore me
gently, at her peaceful, sleepy pace.
So long have the canals been made by now, that
but little if any of the signs of their making remain.
Only for their tideless waters, many of them might
well be rivers—threads of silver on which are strung
the brilliant emeralds of many meadows.

I can well believe that in the days of their incep-
tion they must have seemed the work of Goths and
Vandals in the land.   Indeed, I find a book upon my
shelves—the *Miscellaneous Pieces in Prose* of John
Aikin, M.D., and Anna Lætitia Barbauld—in which
these two amiable collaborators vent their united
spleen upon what they call the evil Genius of the
Canal.

Published in 1792, this little book of essays ran
into its third edition, by which I gather that John
Aikin and his companion, Anna Lætitia, had a large
circle of friends.   I can conceive no one buying the
book but in the cause of friendship.   But good or
bad, it was thus far interesting to me in that it
wrote of canals at so early a date.

It is written in the first person and represents
the sentiments of John Aikin or Anna Lætitia—
perhaps of both.   I like, anyhow, to think that it
was Anna Lætitia.   I will tell you later why.   She
describes herself, on a pleasant evening succeeding a
sultry summer day, as being *invited by Nature* to take
a solitary walk.

I am sure it was Anna Lætitia.

Making her way through the fields and meadows,
she comes to a valley where run both a "small
meandering brook" and "the Duke of Bridgewater's
canal."

"The firm built side of the aqueduct suddenly
opened"—and here I take quotation from the book

itself—" and a gigantic form issued forth, which I soon discovered to be the *Genius of the Canal*. He was clad in a close garment of a russet hue. A mural crown, indented with battlements, surrounded his brow. His naked feet were discoloured with clay. On his shoulder he bore a huge pickaxe, and in his hand he held certain instruments used in surveying and levelling."

Perhaps, after all, it was John Aikin.

This description, however, serves to show you the Genius of the Canal—a spirit with thoughtful looks and features harsh. The *Deity of the Stream* rises from the brook to meet him. Now, the *Deity of the Stream* is habited in a light green mantle—" the clear drops fell from his dark hair, which was encircled with a wreath of water-lily, interwoven with sweet scented flag."

With a contemptuous look and in a hoarse voice, the *Genius of the Canal* addresses the Brook in stern and opprobrious terms.

" Hence, ignoble rill ! " he begins, after which it were not courteous to the imagination to quote the rest. Such a beginning can come to no good end. Concluding, he demands the homage — " due from sloth and obscurity to grandeur and utility."

To which the Brook replies in gentle accents :

" I readily acknowledge the superior magnificence and more extensive utility of which you so proudly

boast ; yet, in my humble walk, I am not void of
a praise, less shining, but not less solid than yours.
The nymph of this peaceful valley, rendered more
fertile and beautiful by my stream ; the neighbouring
sylvan deities, to whose pleasure I contribute, will
pay a grateful testimony to my merit."

Oh, surely it must have been Anna Lætitia.   I
cannot conceive of John Aikin writing this.   He
was of too coarse a mould.

Whichever of the two it was, a strange note
of prophecy is struck in the end on the Brook's
reply.

" And when thy glories, proud Genius ! "—so it
runs—" are lost and forgotten ; when the flood of
commerce, which now supplies thy urn, is turned
into another course and has left thy channel dry
and desolate, the softly flowing Avon shall still
murmur in song, and his banks receive the homage
of all who are beloved by Phœbus and the Muses."

At a time when railways were not even dreamed
of, this was indeed prophetic.   But desolate though
the Thames and Severn Canal now may be, it has
such beauties as I shall ever remember.   Were Anna
Lætitia to stand at the topmost lock of the Golden
Valley, where the Sapperton Tunnel pierces its dark
way into the very heart of the hills, were she to
stand there to-day and look down that wonderful
valley of glorious gold, where in the month of May
the deep woods have laid down their royal carpet

of blue-bells, she must indeed retract all of that little miscellaneous piece of prose she wrote one day, a century ago, when John Aikin perhaps had gone abroad to attend a burial, and Nature had given her gentle invitation to the fields.

X

WHY I WOULD LIKE IT TO HAVE BEEN ANNA LÆTITIA

This is why I would like it to have been Anna Lætitia. One makes pictures in one's mind ; one makes them often from the books one reads. Most vividly there live in my sight the places and the people in the Arabian Nights. No artist, however skilful, could ever change my view of them. I know Herr Teufelsdroeckh as well as I know my own father. I should recognise both as readily in the street. But it is the same with every single one of us. We all have our mental pictures, and the reality can never utterly thrust them from our minds.

Now, my picture of Anna Lætitia was not conceived in my own brain. It was made for me ; and if it was John Aikin who wrote the apologia, then I am all at fault and my picture is not true. But I want it to be true. It amuses me to think it is. And this is the picture—a little triolet, by Frances Cornford.

" O why do you walk through the fields in gloves,
    Missing so much and so much ?
O fat white woman whom nobody loves,
Why do you walk through the fields in gloves,
When the grass is soft as the breast of doves
And shivering sweet to the touch ?
O why do you walk through the fields in gloves,
Missing so much and so much ? "

I am quite sure it must have been Anna Lætitia. And when Nature invited her to take a solitary walk, she put on her best white cambric, her black gloves, and off she went.

Why, of course it must have been Anna Lætitia !

XI

SHIPTON-ON-CHERWELL

THROUGH Port Meadow the canal winds out of Oxford and, until you be past Wolvercote Bridge and Lock, there is little but the sight of those suburbs which are growing like some unsightly fungus around the larger towns of England. That people now, and more and more, should live outside the towns in which their business lies, is in no way to be regretted, but that the property should fall into the hands of those jerry-builders—men of execrable taste, whose only thought is to build for the profit it will bring them in a life-time—this, surely, is a matter for considerable remedy.

With infinite care and trouble we preserve our old buildings; why not with equal care regard our new ?

The fact of the matter is, this is the age of the individualist. A man no longer builds a good house that it may be a pleasant home for his children and his children's children after him. He makes a dwelling which shall serve as profit to himself for just so long as he lives. And it is this instinct of the individualist which, amongst other things, brings about the cheap ornate style of architecture. A man builds a house to catch the vulgar eye. But in days gone past they built simply, because they would build well. A castellated turret is no fit design for a house with a rent of forty pounds a year. At such a price no castellations could be made to withstand the destructive power of time. But with a castellated turret, a residence will twice as soon be let, and so the best and simplest of labour is thrown away upon these abominable appurtenances which only degrade the taste of those who see and live in them.

I remember well, one Mr ——, a jerry-builder in one of the suburbs of London. He threw up rows of villas in a night, as you build a house of cards upon a nursery table. One day I visited him, and was shown into the drawing-room of his own villa— the last and most ornate of a long and vulgar row.

It was papered in a bright and bilious yellow. The chairs were upholstered in plush of rich maroon —a green cloth was upon one table, while on another stood a palm in a pot bound round with scarlet crinkled paper. To complete the last expression of his taste, there was in one corner a drain-pipe of a sky-blue glaze supporting another palm, and prominently upon the yellow walls were two photographs— enlarged to life-size—of himself and his wife. Without one colour of exaggeration, this was and is the home of the jerry-builder—the man who caters for the individualist.

" You're very comfortable here," said I, as he came into the room, his hat pitched back upon his head.

" 'Ere ? " said he ; " well, we don't use this room much 'cept Sundays, when my daughter plays to us a bit on the pianner. It's too nice to use reelly, yer know."

" I should feel inclined myself," said I, " to keep the door locked on it always."

" I know what yer mean," he replied, " it *is* too good for everyday use ; but after all, if yer can afford to buy nice things, I don't see why yer shouldn't be able to enjoy 'em. Nice wallpaper, ain't it ? I can let yer 'ave some of that at"—he paused, doubtless to put on the halfpenny—" at one and ninepence ha'penny the piece."

" That's marvellous ! " I exclaimed.

" What—the price ? "

" No," said I, " the paper."

He said he knew I had good taste, and that was why he had offered it to me.

Now this is the man who has had the greatness thrust upon him of making modern architecture. The fire of London rid us of the plague. What a range of conflagration should we need to rid us of the jerry-builder !

Until you make Wolvercote, then, you will see his handiwork at every turn of the canal ; but after that comes the rich broad country. Then the willows begin to draw down to the water's edge,

bending and stooping like thirsty cattle to drink their
fill.   Their twisted fantastic roots dip deep into the
cool water.   I never wonder when I see a group of
willows that Arthur Rackham should find them to

shape into a thousand fairies and dryads.   Indeed,
there is a personality in every tree—a giant in the
oak, a ploughman in the elm, a princess in the poplar,
a knight-errant with his plume and armour in the
pine ; but the pollard willow, she is the home of the
water sprite, the dryad and the nymph.   Every branch

is a fairy's arm with tapering fingers, playing strange music on the pipes of the wind.

For the first hour or so out of Oxford, I thought surely I had come on a fool's errand.

"My God," said I to myself in despair, "Anna Lætitia was right!" and, putting both hands to my mouth, I called out to Eynsham Harry.

"Is it like this all the way?" I cried.

He left his horse. She stopped at once to nibble by the hedge.

"Is the canal like this all the way?" I asked him as he came back along the path.

"Oh no, sur," said he: "look you, there's fine country soon as you come past Thrupp."

"And where shall we stop for the night?"

"Well, that's as it likes you, sur. We reach Shipton Church 'bout seven this evening. There be a good flow of water under, and we shall make Shipton Church 'bout seven."

"Right away, then," said I. "Go along as fast as you can till we get away from these damned red brick villas."

By which you may see I was mildly endeavouring to live up to the reputation of the bargee—a reputation for strong language which, so long as I have known him, he has utterly failed to fulfil.

"I suppose you like the old houses best?" said Eynsham Harry as he moved away.

"I do," said I: "don't you?"

" Well, sur," he replied, " I don't know that it has much to do wi' me, anyway.   I couldn't stop in a house, look you ; I should catch cold the first night. 'Tis the same wi' any of us used to living on the boats.   I haven't slept out of a boat since I was born."

Indeed, I can well understand it.   These small cabins on the barges are as snug as they can be. A panel of one wall lets down, meeting across to the other side, and there is your bed as comfortable as that in many an hotel.   When swung up again, the cabin is easily capacious enough for two, though often with these families it will accommodate more.   In the same fashion as the bed, the door of a cupboard lets down to form a table.   At the foot of the cabin steps, with chimney protruding through the roof, a small stove provides all that is necessary for warmth and cooking.   Not an inch of the space is wasted.   There are cupboards everywhere for clothes, crockery, and everything you need.

As I took the tiller again and we swung off once more into the centre of the road, I heard the old clock ticking softly in the cabin below me. At that moment the birds of one accord had ceased their singing, and except for the even, monotonous stepping of Eynsham Harry's horse, this was the only sound in all the stillness.

At Thrupp we came to the first of those draw-bridges which the mere weight of a man will raise to let the barge pass through.   At first I thought

Eynsham Harry would never be there in time to swing her up for the barge's passage. But they know to a moment, these men—as well, indeed, they should —how long it takes. Not one instant, neither too soon nor too late, did he leave the horse's head. With sagging tow-line she walked calmly on, crossing the bridge after him to the tow-path on the other side. Then, almost as the nose of the *Flower of Gloster* passed into the shadow, he had caught hold

of the big arms, lifted himself off his feet, and up swung the bridge like a feather lifted on the wind.

These bridges are characteristic of Oxfordshire. You meet with them in no other county than this. They join, as often as not, the low-lying meadows which the canal intersects, and are mostly set down with their great arms stretching upward to admit of the access of cattle from one field to another.

Immediately after passing that at Thrupp, where there is a little cluster of old Oxfordshire cottages

and a farm, the canal takes a sudden, almost rect-
angular turn.   Here it leads in a straight reach down
to the church of Shipton village, which stands upon
the river Cherwell.

In reality the canal is nearer to the village than
the river ; but in the days when Shipton-on-Cherwell
received its name, they knew of no canal, nor dreamed
of its existence.

It was here, in the long rushes that grow under the
broad elm trees, that we moored the *Flower of Gloster*,
and Eynsham Harry took the horse over the bridge
up into the village to find her stabling for the night.

XII

SHIPTON-ON-CHERWELL—*continued*

In the vale of the Cherwell lies the little village of
Shipton, the first hamlet of interest you will come to
out of Oxford. The graveyard of the church rises
from the canal's edge, and at the top of the high
mound—a hill it were foolish to call it—stands the
church with its square Norman tower under the deep
shadows of thick elms.

There I spent the first evening of my journey,
and for many a year shall remember it. It had been
one of those long hot days in May when the sun in
a blue heaven has warmed the ground and all the
water beneath its rays. A hatch of fly had come out
upon the canal and, as the sun set, while Eynsham
Harry was away in the village, I seated myself on
the cabin roof of the *Flower of Gloster*, watching the
low-flying swallows feed from the surface of the
water.

Up from the bridge, down to the corner they
sped and back again. Their flight was like that of
some arrow with steel-blue head, shot low from its

Shipton-on-Cherwell.

cross-bow. Dipping on the surface, they rose again, leaving faint ripples that spread into ever-widening circles as they melted into the smoothness of the water once more. Just as this, might an arrow ricochet off the water in its flight. Then, as they swerved upwards to the turn, I caught the swift warm gleam of pink upon their throats. As swiftly it vanished when they dipped again and flashed by me once more.

Someone told me the other day that the modern aeronaut finds much to criticise in the flight of a swallow.

" With that construction," says he, " the swallow should not be able to fly as easily as she does."

I have no doubt that this may be so. It is conceivable that, built as she is, the swallow should by no right fly so beautifully. But if aeroplanes be the proper method of flying, then I know as little of aeronautics as must God have done when first He made the swallow. One day, perhaps, I shall meet the flautist who will tell me that the white-throat which sang to me all that evening in an elder tree upon the other bank has no conception as to how to produce his notes. And doubtless he will be perfectly right as well. We know so much nowadays ; so much more than ever we did. Look at my window-cleaner at Oxford ! I am sure that Lairs and Penaits was not the full extent of his knowledge of the dead languages. In fact, I should think the only thing he did not know in this world was how to clean a window. And you can rub along quite easily without this accomplishment—especially if it be your trade.

I am content, however, with the flight of a swallow. I even approve of those few unvaried notes of the white-throat which over and over again she sang to me that evening from her elder tree.

It must have been well-nigh an hour I sat there before Eynsham Harry returned. And if I sat quite still, the wagtails came fearlessly down from the bridge under which they were a-building. They were more busy than I have ever been in my life. I thought that then—what amazing industry there is in all Nature! It is only man who, having measured out Time upon the dial of a clock, knows how to waste it; and I rather suspect that that invention of the chronometer has been his downfall. The moment he discovered that he could divide a day into hours, he began to temporise, and the first clock that rang its chime heralded the birth of procrastination. It is this way, with his endless wisdom, that a man is always making his own Frankenstein.

But in the animal world there is no other time-keeper than Necessity. Now, you cannot temporise with that. That is why the wagtails worked so hard, stepping swiftly with their dainty feet over the light surface of the mud. That is why the swallows

never ceased their flying to and fro the canal.
When I thought of it—all that day they had been
upon the wing ! Such tireless labour, if he could
but achieve it, might make the threescore years and
ten of a man more worthy of its record when his day
had reached its end.

" I am tired," some man caused to be written
for his epitaph—" I am tired of all this buttoning and
unbuttoning."

That he should have unbuttoned at last to so
good a purpose as that truthful jest, excuses him of
much of the time he wasted. But there are many
of us who button and unbutton every day with no
greater purpose to ourselves and others as just serves
to keep us in the bounds of decency. But what is a
day of decency to one hour slipped away ? The
swallow obeys that Nature which has been given him
and earns no criticism from any one of us. Why,
even on the canals, where circumstance makes no
allowance for it, the ordinary so-called laws of
decency are held in no regard. And no sense of yours
is violated then.

I spoke of this matter one day to Eynsham Harry
—I spoke of it with some reserve, yet spoke of it
because I wished to know.

" What do the women of the barge do in such
cases," I asked, " when you are miles from any
cottage or place of habitation ? "

" Do ? " said he. " Why, look you, sur—that

hedge which runs along by every tow-path.   If
Nature couldn't grow enough leaves on that hedge
to hide a sparrow's nest, it ain't no good to God, man,
nor beast."

I wanted no better answer than that.   Where
there is Nature there are no laws of decency.   Not
only to the physiologist, but to Nature too, all things
are pure.

XIII

SHIPTON-ON-CHERWELL—*continued*

SEEING that one of these fine days I must lie buried
somewhere, and it being best to speak of such things
while one has a voice in the matter, then of all places
let me lie under the shadow of the elms in Shipton
churchyard.

It rises in a sudden slope from the canal's edge
and surrounds the church on the crest of the mound.
In the early part of May, when first I visited it, the
high, thick grass was dotted with cuckoo flowers from
the midst of which the moss-grown grave-stones just
rose in unobtrusive memory of those who lay beneath.
Nearly all the raised mounds of earth, often so sadly
reminiscent of the shapes of the bodies they cover,
were concealed in the long grass ; but where one was
exposed, there lifted the scarlet head of a tulip as
though to prove how full of life is that acre which
belongs to God.

When I returned in the last week of the month
it was all changed.   From the plain, pink muslin of her
cuckoo flower, spring had put on her gorgeous lace

The Churchyard.

blossoms of heracleum. The whole place was white
and feathered with their blooms. Scarcely above them,
then, rose the silent heads of the grave-stones. Often
you must push the blossoms aside to read the names
of those who lay beneath. And above it all, like a
sentinel guarding the peace of those good country
folk who slept there, the tower of the old Norman
church rose out of the thick branches of the elms and
faced the sky.

> When the night comes for me to rest,
> Let me lie down in the long green grass.
> I need no garden with fine flowers dressed
> When the night comes for me to rest ;
> Where Nature sows I shall sleep best,
> And where God reaps no place surpass.
> When the night comes for me to rest,
> Let me lie down in the long green grass.

At Shipton House, which stands just next to and
above the churchyard, they told me that once King
John had had his garden. Dr Yule, who lies buried in
a vault beside the church, has no doubt written of this
in the papers he compiled concerning the history of
Shipton. I called at the vicarage there, in the hope
of being allowed to see them, but the vicar was at
Oxford for the day, and, writing later, he was possibly
still away in Oxford, for I received no reply. In any
case, it is not wise to let valuable papers out of one's
hands, and that to the first vagabond who happens to
come along.

As I walked up the drive to the vicarage door, there were some jolly children playing on the lawn white with daisies. A little dog left his frolicking with them and came to tell me that I was nothing less than an intruder.

> "Hark, hark, the dogs do bark,
>   The beggars are coming to Town."

That little nursery rhyme ran inevitably in my head as I rang the bell. Of course, the vicar was quite right not to answer my letter.

But if he had, I might have written more of the history of Shipton, of which I am assured there is no little to be told. And yet, this is no guide-book, so perhaps it is as well without. I only loved the place as I saw it with its elm trees and its cow-parsnips—the old Roman cross that stands solitary in the grave-yard, and all those wild flowers of the field which combine to make it one of the most restful spots I have ever seen.

For some hours that night I lay awake listening to the great silence. No doubt it was the first strangeness of that bed in the cabin of the *Flower of Gloster* which kept me from sleeping. But it was a rest to lie there, nevertheless. Through the open door-way of the cabin the stars were glittering in a deep-blue sky, and now and then a bird chirped sleepily as its mate pressed close against it on the branch.

"A man might do worse," thought I, "than

spend his life like this." But when I began to con-
sider how it might be done, I fell asleep.

The next morning we started at five. I was
sitting on the roof of the cabin eating my breakfast
as we passed through Heyford Lock.

XIV

SOMERTON

ALL that day we wound through the meadows. The cattle came down to the water's edge to look at us as we passed. They are shy, curious things, young heifers. The world is very new to them. In their

soft eyes is all that patient wonder of the child. So near did we pass them at times that, had I swung the tiller round, I might have touched their noses with my hand.

So the day slips, just as the meadows pass, in that silent, gliding way whereby it is gone before you have thought to count an hour of it. Only now and again is the pleasant monotony of it broken by the commotion of a passing barge. Then there is cracking of whips, the raising of voices, the soft scraping purr as the boat runs by you, touching your side. Scraps of conversation are exchanged ere they shoot out of distance and, turning some sudden corner, are lost to sight. For a long while before, you may often hear them coming. Where there is none to lead the horse, a man will sit at the tiller with his whip, cracking it ever and again as the gentle beast lingers to nibble from the hedge. Nearer grows that sound and nearer, until the smoking funnel from the cabin fire can just be seen above the hedgerows. Then round she swings into sight—a Fellows Morton with a load of straw, a pair of Falkeners with cargoes of best bright, or a Shropshire Union with her odorous merchandise of gas-water.

Sometimes perhaps it is a fly-boat out of Birmingham, travelling her steady three miles an hour, day and night, like the old express coaches of a time that few of us are now left to remember. One and all they know each other's journeys, as sailors will tell you in mid-ocean the destination of some passing vessel; as ships too, they will hail each other in passing while the tow-lines swing across.

"Good morning, Joseph!"

"Good morning, Harry!"

"If 'ee see Sam in Oxford, tell 'en I 've got that there horse for 'en whenever he wants to see 'er."

And then no doubt may follow little scraps of canal gossip in voices rising as the distance increases between them. For never do they loiter. Time is a precious matter with them, and with them also necessity is their chronometer. They are like the wagtails. Often I envied them the hours they spent a-working.

At Somerton that second day, I had lunch at a little inn by the canal side ; indeed *I* might  loiter as I chose. It was while the good lady was making ready—the boiled eggs, the glass of beer, the piece of cheese —that I strolled up into the village with its grey stone cottages and neat, trim gardens. A Norman church is here as well. Eynsham Harry came with me, and together we secured the keys. A youth of twelve, of a suspicious turn of mind, was deputed to carry them and accompany us.

For a moment I stood looking at the Tower before we entered.

" Nine hundred years odd seems very little when you look at that," said I.

Eynsham Harry stood and stared at it.

" Is it nine hundred years since that was built ? " he asked presently.

" It is indeed," said I—" there or thereabouts."

" Well," he added after a pause—" I 'old wi' churches in their proper place."

But what he meant by it, I cannot attempt to say.

By this time the boy was waiting at the door, and in we went, whereupon the boy followed us closely, watching all we did. I fancy he was more deeply suspicious of me. I think, moreover, he was right. With a rich and a poor man, I would always mistrust the rich. There is only one reason why a poor man steals—the pain of extreme need.

Beyond that, there is nothing so honest as poverty. Now, of the two of us, my poverty was the least apparent. It came, no doubt, of having a coloured tie, a gold watch-chain, and a crease to my trousers. It was not a crease that lasted for long ; but this was only my second day. I have no doubt, however, that Eynsham Harry is a richer man than I am.

When I found the youth at our heels in the chancel, I turned on him.

" What are you afraid we'll steal ? " I asked.

" There be'ant nothin' to steal," he replied—" 'tis all lockit up."

I asked him why, and he told me that two weeks before an old silver chalice had been stolen, by visitors, from the altar. I can conceive no theft more meanly done than this. One might never say a prayer in a church from one year's end to another and be little the worse for it ; but to steal from the

high altar—were it only a flower at harvest-time—
must be the greatest of all deadly sins, whether it be
included in the seven or no.

But this guarding the stable when the horse was
locked up somewhere else was characteristic of the
precaution of country life. I could not help but
smile. The boy followed our every footstep, and the
moment we had gone out locked the door again,
taking the coppers I gave him with a pull at his
forelock.

Back at the inn where we had lunch, I found a
book, the title of which attracted me. "A Book on
Etiquette, by a Member of the Aristocracy."

"Is it etiquette," said I, "to announce in print
that you are a member of that much-to-be-envied
class of people?"

Eynsham Harry set a piece of cheese upon his
knife and shook his head.

"Let's see what he has to say about it": whereupon I opened the book and read.

"When entertaining guests," says this member
of the aristocracy—or it is words to this effect—"do
not produce the family album and expect them to be
interested in the portraits of people whom they have
never met. Rather keep them amused and interested
by light and chatty conversation, so that they will
feel the time pass easily until it is the proper moment
to take their leave."

I wonder how many trusting people have taken

to heart these words of a member of the aristocracy, putting away their splendid albums wherein
the photo of Uncle William taken in Toronto in a
violent thunderstorm always made everyone laugh
who looked at it ?   I wonder how many dull evenings
that member of the aristocracy is accountable for,
when the poor hostess strives a thousand times to
begin a light and chatty conversation and, failing
utterly, falls to silence, yet still refrains from bringing
down that leather-covered volume with its nickel-
silver clasp ?

It is not fair when you are a member of the
aristocracy to take such advantage of your power as
this.   There is only one thing to be done.   Let
some honest merchant in the suburbs write a book
and call it a Book on Sincerity by a Member of the
Democracy.   Only it would never repay him, and I
am sure that book on etiquette was a gold-mine.

XV

THE TRADE IN OLD BITS

" Ride-a-cock horse
To Banbury Cross
To see a fine lady on a white hoss."

INDEED you must say—hoss.   There is scarce a child
of any discrimination who would listen to you if you
did not.   I wonder—

without any of that
sentiment about it at
all which so many people
dislike in others and
enjoy so much in them-
selves—I wonder how
many little pink fingers
have been pinched, how
many little crumpled toes have been pressed to the
concluding lines of that well-worn nursery stanza?
Many and many a million, and doubtless there will
be many a million more.

That was indeed a literary achievement to write
but one stanza which, for so many centuries, should

74

be sung to the race which is to be ; a stanza, moreover, bringing with it those wonderful echoes of youth to every grown-up man and woman who inevitably repeat it to themselves whenever they hear the name of Banbury Town. It may have been of political significance once. So far as I know, the real history of the rhyme has never been traced. But the women of England have found other uses for it, and I am sure they know best.

We came into Banbury that evening where, leaving the barge to Eynsham Harry, I went up into the town. He needed to go no further than some public-house such as the Nag's Head in Oxford. There are always inns ready to the canal to supply the needs of the barges passing continually backwards and forwards. I left him there and hurried up into the town before the shops should close.

There is little of the old aspect of Banbury left now. Agricultural advancement—as indeed with advancement of any sort—has set upon it the seal of the new order of things. A few of the old houses remain ; a few of the old inns. Old arches beneath the houses will often invite you to stop and look within ; but as often as not they are disappointing. The Reindeer Inn still has its beauties. The shop in Parson's Street dating at least, so I am informed, from the year 1616, still sells the famous cakes made from the old recipe, and still keeps the odour of its years about it. They even retain the

old windows, just as they were, against all the tempting advantages of plate-glass.

The new cross which stands in the market-place
was erected in 1858 to commemorate the marriage
of the Princess Royal with the Crown Prince of
Prussia.   I do not think it pretends in any way to be
a copy of the old, or even to occupy the original site.
It is two centuries and a half ago since the Puritans
destroyed it.   I often wonder where vandalism ends
and religious zeal begins.   It must be a fine line indeed that separates them.

But were I bent upon giving a history of the
Town of Banbury or of any other place upon the
road, this chronicle of the *Flower of Gloster* had never
been written.   What happens to you upon a voyage
of discovery is that you learn the world by what you
see and not by what you hear.

Indeed I saw little in Banbury, for, to tell the
truth, the cross greatly disappointed me, and neither
appetite nor curiosity were strong enough to persuade
me to the cakes.   Beyond these, is there anything
in Banbury but legend and fairy-tale ?   There are
numbers of windows filled with the glaring modernity
of agricultural instruments.   No doubt they have
grown into their place in the field ; they have become
part of the soil upon which they work.   The whirr of
the reaper is now a sound that one has learnt to
associate with those still, hot days of late summer.
It is as natural to the ear now as the note of the corn-

crake. I would not lose it for the world. But, displayed as they were in the streets of Banbury, I felt them somehow out of place.

As I stood and looked at them, I thought of that farmer in the south of Ireland, when first he brought the reaper and binder into his fields. He had only hired the machine. So delicate and intricate an instrument was beyond his means to buy. He had only hired it, and stood there in his cornfield with me as slowly and surely it narrowed down the swaying army of blades of wheat. I watched the wonder in his eyes as the relentless arms swept down their burden against the knives, as, load by load, they gathered it into sheaves, bound it and cast it from them. For a long while he never spoke. He watched it silently with a breathless interest—a conscript thrust unwillingly into the invading ranks of time.

At last he turned to me.

"Shure, 'tis the divil in ut!" said he. "Mind ye, 'tis no surprise to me the way ut reaps at all, but how the hell does ut tie the knot in the shtring? There must be fingers to do ut—faith, 'twill take me all me time to tie a knot meself, but that damn thing does ut wid its eyes shut. I don't like the ways of ut at all."

That was just what I felt when I saw the agricultural machines in Banbury; but it was the looks and not the ways of them I disliked. And that was not the only thing which spoilt my impression of the Town. I went into a curio shop there. Where,

indeed, did I not go into a curio shop ?   In most of
them is that inimitable atmosphere of age.   The
world has a history to it in these places ; but in this
curio shop there was none.   All the brass candlesticks and bed-warmers looked unreal.

" Is this old brass ? " I asked of the man who
served me.

" Every bit of it," he replied with confidence.

I picked up a box, purporting to be one of those old
candle boxes which have come to us from Flanders.

" This old ? " said I.

" Oh—yes—oh, yes," said he—" we don't touch
anything but old bits."

I examined it, and found that the hinges were
new.   The solder joining it together was as fresh as
paint ; the very edges were sharp.   No hands had
ever lifted that lid when the long winter evenings
were drawing in.   No tallow candles had ever lain
there waiting to be used.   It was all redolent of the
agricultural machine, and there was no soil of which
it could become a part.

" How much do you want for it ? " I asked.

" Twenty-five shillings."

I smiled.   In Birmingham where it had been
made, probably it had cost two.   Now, when he saw
me smile, thinking too perhaps from the way I had
examined it that I knew more than I really do, he
made a generous, nay, a flattering offer.

" Twenty shillings to you, sir," said he.

"You know it's not old," said I. "You know it was made last week with seventy others in Birmingham ?"

"Had it eighteen months myself," he replied.

I replied that it.was older than I thought ; but still I pressed my point.

"But you know it is not really old," I persisted.

"I believe it's made up from old brass," said he.

I laughed. I could not help it. I laughed aloud at that.

"Why—my God !" said I, "all brass is old—as old as the metals from which it is made, since they're as old as the earth they come from. Made up of old brass ! Now, supposing I hadn't known any better, would you have let me purchase that believing it to be old ?"

"Why not ?" he replied. "If you hadn't asked, why should I have told you ?"

"Then I take it," said I, "that your idea of the truth is the contradiction of a lie. You must tell your lie first."

"Whose telling lies ?" he demanded.

"Well—one of us," said I, "is telling the truth. I shouldn't like to hurt your feelings by saying which of us it was."

He followed me to the door with the old bit in his hand. I don't think I should care to be a trader in old bits. The world is so full of fools, and every fool is a temptation to a would-be honest man.

XVI

CROPREDY

It was after leaving Banbury that the interest of the journey scarcely ever faltered. Had I really known what travelling was until I went aboard the *Flower of Gloster*? I scarcely think so. The member of Parliament in the early part of the last century who complained that it was a tempting of all Providence to ride upon any vehicle exceeding the speed of twenty miles an hour, has all my respect, if so be it he was speaking of travelling. This insensate desire to get there takes all meaning from the verb " to travel." Indeed, in these days it would seem that the only effort of a man is to conquer the dimensions, to annihilate Space, to crush Time beneath his heel. For man is becoming a socialist not only in matters political ; he would deny even the monarchy of Nature, dethroning that by which alone he may come into his kingdom.

But in the name of Heaven, what has this to do with barges ? Yet, if a man must travel from London to Birmingham in a few odd number of minutes, let

him at least once in his life take a barge from Oxford
and do it in five days.   It will teach him much, and,
amongst other things, he may find that the dimension
of Time is not to be conquered by beating.

We started late out of Banbury that next morning.
I must confess it, I lay long in bed, and not all the
sounds of other barges slipping their lines could
waken me.

When at last I did get up, I gathered from
Eynsham Harry that the other boatmen had been
laughing at him for the strenuous labour of his
journey.

" They say you'd make a fine master for a fly
boat, sur," he told me.

" One man's meat," said I ; " but it's past belief
that any man could find this life a poisoning, even if
he were to travel night and day."

" Well, sur," he replied—and here I learnt he
had by way of a philosophy—" men have peculious
ideas of how they shall enjoy themselves, and they
most ways signifies what sort of men they are.   'Tis
one man in a thousand as chooses in this world what
he shall be, but every jack one of 'em select their
own enjoyment.   I had a week in London once, and
there was a friend of mine what spent every evening
going to a theater.   I've never thought properly of
him since."

I thought softly of the times that I had been to
the theatre, but said no word of it.   I share that

weakness in common with many, that at all hazards I would be thought properly of. Moreover, there was a note in Eynsham Harry's voice which made me feel that, in what he said, there was a point of view which it might take more than logic to destroy. There was more than the Nonconformist conscience to it. I doubt, in fact, whether it were a matter of

conscience at all, for he was not a man to be worried much by trifles.

"Well, how," said I, "do you find your enjoyment?"

He was taking the tiller, making his morning ablutions at the same time, while I lay stretched upon the cabin roof. Fanny, the horse, was ambling quietly along the tow-path, just keeping the line from sagging in the water whenever I had the energy to crack the whip.

Eynsham Harry dried the soap-suds out of the corners of his eyes before he answered me.

"Well, sur," he replied, "as I said before, what I calls enjoyment another man may find little but a waste of time; but, look you, so long as it enjoys me, where's the call to fret about it? If I've got

any time on me hands just about this season of the
year, I can't do no better with myself than go birds-
nesting."

I had thought of—oh! I had thought of everything but that.

"Birds-nesting!" said I. "Have you got a
collection of eggs?"

"No, sur—I had when I was a boy. When I
was a youngster I used to think there was no sense
in goin' a-nesting, not unless I took the eggs. I
don't touch 'en now."

"Why not?"

"Well, 'tis all right in young fellers. I don't
stop my son a-doin' it. But if he takes more than
one egg out of a nest, I give 'en a thrashing. 'Tis
all right with young fellers. They want some sort
to boast about. 'Tis proper for them to have the
feelin's of competition. But, God bless me, I don't
mind if a man knows more about birds 'n what I do.
All I feels is I'd be damn glad to have a talk wi' 'en."

"So you get just as much amusement in finding
the nest, though you don't touch the eggs?

"Every bit, sur. I came back last Sunday week,
and I said to my boy : 'Sunny,' said I, 'I found a
red-start's nest this morning—four eggs.' 'Where,
dad?' says he; 'I haven't got a red-start's.' 'No,
not in your collection,' said I, 'but I've got four in
mine. And you won't learn nothing about the ways
of that bird—not if I tells you where her nest is.

'Taint no sense in buyin' eggs. You find 'en, and then you'll know something you didn't know before.'"

When a man makes you think, there is more than just something to him. From this moment to the end of the journey, I never regretted that thirty shillings a week which had been cajoled out of me in the private parlour of the Nag's Head. Had it been but to learn just this one characteristic of him, the thirty shillings were worth it.

For some little while, then, I sat looking on ahead to where Fanny was quietly making her journey. Every moment she would shuffle a step nearer to the edge, casting a wistful glance at the young, green shoots of the hawthorn. Another step nearer, and at the crack of my whip she would fall back into the tow-path's centre with a dropping of her ears, well knowing she had been found out.

"Then I suppose," said I presently, "you don't like London?"

"I do not, sur—there's no Nature in the place. 'Tis all people. And I holds when you get all people and no Nature it ain't natural. 'Tis Nature what gives us something to be doin', and when you've got none of it, then people invents their enjoyments out of their own heads. I've heard tell they do queer thin's in London. I've heard tell there are women at the theaters there what dance wi' scarce no clothes on them, and that people come in thousands to see 'en. I've heard they go putting themselves into positions as any woman would feel shame to be seen in, and that ladies go wi' gentlemen to watch 'en. Now, look you, sur, they wouldn't do that if birds built nesties in London."

The amazing amount of truth in so preposterous a statement almost bewildered me.

"You go up to London," said I, "and say that where people can hear you."

" 'Tis no affair of mine, sur," said he quietly.
" They ain't my children, or I'd thrash 'en."

I laughed.   I pictured Eynsham Harry thrashing
the countess of——

"But it's a strange thing," I went on presently—
" you know the boys of the present generation are
losing all their interest in Nature.   The modern
school-boy no longer spends his half-holidays in
birds-nesting.   There's scarcely one of 'em knows
anything about geology.   Collections amongst the
school-boys now are matters of business.   They
collect stamps only to sell at a profit.   We're becoming worse than a nation of shopkeepers.   We're a
nation of pawnbrokers now, pledging everything we
have for the sake of an appearance of wealth.   I've
watched the boys at Wellington College.   When
they come out of school for their half-holidays, they
go straight away to a hosier's shop and buy the latest
thing in socks, the smartest thing in ties.   They go
to the barber's and get their hair neatly trimmed and
scented.   Why, I remember when I was at school,
if a boy had scent on his hair, my God, he never forgot it ! "

" I don't know nothin' about that," said Eynsham
Harry.   " I never went to school myself."

" But you can read and write ? " said I.

" Not a word," said he.   " All those poster things
on the hoardings as we come into Birningame mean
nothin' to me."

" I've always thought," said I, " that there were many drawbacks to education. Then you know nothing of what you should add to the homely salutation of good-morning ? "

" No—good-morning is enough for me," he replied.

" It should be enough for anyone," said I.

At this moment, while he was looking in the cabin mirror, brushing his hair, I took the tiller and straightway, being more concerned with our conversation than any matter of steering, I ran her nose full tilt into a built-up side of the bank.

" By God," said he with a laugh, " that gave her Warwick ! It only shows you, sur, that we must have been talkin' very foolish."

It was quite pleasing, that childish sense of fatality. There was the best of Calvinism in it.

A moment later we took a sharp turn under a bridge, and there were the black arms of lock-gates stretched out to greet us.

" What place is this ? " I asked as I saw the cluster of red-tiled roofs that spoke a village.

" This is Cropredy, sur—Cropredy Bridge. We'll just get through the lock and stop a bit. I always go here to the Red Lion for a drink."

XVII

THE FIRST PATCHWORK
QUILT—CROPREDY

To the Red Lion we went, leaving the *Flower of Gloster* moored by the bank on the far side of the lock ; giving Fanny her nose-bag, for which she made a pair of big dark eyes blink gratefully.

These country inns with their floors of sawdust, their old lead-lighted windows through which the sunlight falls and makes the floor a chequer-board of gold, they always delight me. It is here of an evening you learn something about the land you live in. The boards of the trestled tables bear the ill-cut names of many a one who has laid down the law and told the Prime Minister in a few straight words just what he thought of him.

In the middle of the morning, when the men are away working in the fields and the parlour is empty, what a place to sit in, to call for a glass of beer, a plate of cheese, ere you set forth again upon the journey you may be taking ! To some inns there are small gardens set out with their patchwork of

flowers.   Where they face upon a street, as did the
Red Lion of Cropredy then, as often as not a jug of
flowers stands out upon the window-sill.   They are
a patchwork collection, too.   Country people never
put one kind of flower in a vase by itself.   They
mix them all up—roses and daisies, Canterbury bells
and geraniums, all are thrust together in one multi-
coloured mass.   That is their idea of colour—a patchwork.   They know nothing of chromatic scales, of
tones that blend or harmonies that meet.   They mix
their flowers as they see God mix His.   That is good
enough for them.   It is a patchwork.

It was an old woman far away in the heart of the
country, as you may fancy, who first thought of a
patchwork quilt.   No artist could ever have thought
of that.   It was an old, old woman with a twinkle
of laughter in her eye and a child's love of colour in
her heart.

One day, when first she was wed, she burnt a hole
in her red flannel petticoat.   It was only a small hole,
but when she picked up her skirt to cross the road on a
muddy day, she felt all the neighbours' eyes upon it.
So she cut a square piece out and stitched another in.
There was that neatness about it, you could never have
seen where it was done.

Now what was the good of the piece she had cut
out ?   None at all !   But it was excellent flannel.   If
you want to know the truth of the matter, she had
bought that petticoat for her wedding morning.

Wasn't it a pity to throw it away ? Well—she saved it.

That was the birth of the patchwork quilt.

Along with that piece of flannel, which was tucked away in the deep corner of a drawer, there was added

a square piece out of the seat of her husband's trousers. And so, piece by piece, increasing in numbers as the family increased, the material of the ultimate patchwork quilt was slowly harvested in that drawer. But what she was ever to do with them, that she could never have said. Necessity decided that for her ; for it is Necessity who is the greatest craftsman amongst men.

They grew old and they grew poor.   And as they grew old, they felt the chill of winter the more ; and as they grew poor, they had not clothes sufficient upon their bed to warm them.

It was then she thought of her pieces that now filled the recess of that old drawer.   Necessity whispered it in her ear and, picking up her needle, she began to sew.   In a week the patchwork quilt was made ; and in the early mornings when they lay awake, in all seriousness her husband would point out a patch to her and say :

" Mother—where di that coom from ? "

" That," said she, " were the tail out of our Johnny's first little shirt."

This is one of the beauties of a real patchwork quilt.   For these are the things that really keep you warm.

XVIII

THE RED LION—CROPREDY

ALMOST from the canal's edge a little street runs up, with a row of Tudor cottages on one side and the high wall of the grave-yard on the other. This is the village of Cropredy. A few outlying houses there are, of course, a farmstead here, there the vicarage ; but this little street is Cropredy. Down this street the horses of the Cavaliers galloped one day with a brave rattling of harness and the wind in their plumes. You cannot but feel that little has changed since then. Only the canal is there, which in those days was never dreamed of. But so long has it been in existence now, so long have the barges been passing to and fro, that even that seems part of the place.

It is in the midst of this row of cottages that you will find the Red Lion. To the gentlest breeze, a red sign-board swings outside, adding another instrument to the orchestra of sounds which are inseparable from the country village. I wish to hear no better music than the symphonies which Nature plays upon her countless instruments.

When we walked into the parlour, two farm- 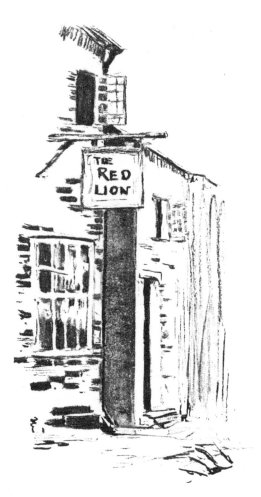 hands were already there. On their way from one field to another, they had chosen a path which must lead them through the village ; and the sign of the Red Lion had swung backwards and forwards, singing its song of invitation. Where is the man who would not have stepped within ? Their pints of ale were on the trestle table. The sun was shining a rich amber through the rough glass mugs. Their arms, bared to the elbow, were burnt and brown. The sawdust of the floor never looked so clean.

"Good mornin'!" said they—"fine mornin'."

What club is there in London where a man, if he did not know you, would say as much? What club is there would provide the entertainment we had there then?

Upon the wall opposite the open fireplace there was a board, marked out as a sun-dial, each division bearing the value of some number. A ring in the centre marked the highest number of all. The board was painted black, and all about the face of it were little holes where darts had entered. It was a game they played to wile away a lazy hour.

At Eynsham Harry's invitation, we played with them then—played for four glasses of ale, while the landlord in his apron leaned within the doorway, keeping the score with a piece of chalk, pleasantly content whoever won or lost.

And the glass of ale that followed! I can see the sun sparkling in it now. Each one of us as we raised it to our lips muttered "Good Health"— and not only wished, but felt it.

Is there any club in London where, upon your first entrance, old members would treat you with such good comradeship as this?

For every meaning of a club, there is no place to touch the village inn. Here a man upon his entrance s straightway at one with all the company—a good fellow until he proves that he is not. A gentle thirst is the only qualification for membership, and it black-balls no one. Not a rule is written, but every law is tacitly obeyed. A man expels himself. There is none of the terrible formality of compulsory resignation. If he is not liked, he does not enter the club. He condemns himself. It is only the hyper-civilised conditions of modern life which make these things impossible. In the city you must make your rules and print them ; but in the country, they take their laws from Nature, the book of which is spread open in the fields that those who run may read.

Maintenance work in progress on the Thames and Severn Canal near Bowbridge

The Thames and Severn Canal at Chalford looking east (top) and west

XIX

THE HISTORY OF CROPREDY

HAD I meant to be chronicler of anything beside my journey in the *Flower of Gloster*, doubtless I should have left the history of Cropredy alone. But the best of a chronicle of this nature is that you may set out with one intention and, before you have gone a mile or more upon your journey, find yourself in passing company with another.

To speak of the history of any place is much in the spirit of the guide's litany ; but when I sat alone on the lawn of the vicarage garden and read the brief history of Cropredy from the papers which the vicar was good enough to give me, I said to myself, "This is not wonderful—it's true."

There are no astounding figures of height and breadth and depth, therefore I have no desire to astonish you with the year of our Lord. It is the year of our Lord—if you will have it so—1911, and the village of Cropredy has been asleep for two hundred and sixty-seven years.

Two hundred and sixty-seven years ago, they

fought the battle of Cropredy Bridge. But even two years before then, the king's standard was set up at Edgecot, and all around Cropredy, in the meadows, the king's army slept the night before Edgehill.

I should like to have been sitting that night in the parlour of the Red Lion. I would have liked to have heard the songs of the Cavaliers as they heralded the coming of the morning.

> "King Charles! Who's for a fight now?
> King Charles! Who'll do him right now?"

The greatest poet of the last century knew well the lilt of them.

But it was two years later, in 1644, that Cropredy heard the music of the clash of arms, the thunder of battle. Eleven cannon and fourteen small brass and leather guns were taken on that day. And Colonel Weymes was made a prisoner. You have only to stand on Cropredy Bridge, with the meadows at either side of you, to see it all; you have only to walk up the cobbled pavement in the little street to know what a day that was in the history of Cropredy.

Even now, they still dig up cannon shot, soldiers' buttons, and rusty swords when the blade of the plough throws back the secretive earth. In the churchyard itself there are two tombstones bearing each the inscription, "A faithful soldier of King Charles ye First." Indeed, the next day after the battle—so the records of the church will inform you—

it was the vicar's duty to bury five soldiers. Only these two of their tombstones remain.

I think I should like to be a vicar in some country parish in England. The peace and quietness of those vicarage gardens, walled snugly off from the old church, are ideal corners of the world. It must, too, be a great thing to tell people what you think of them, at least once in every week ; to sit at ease in your own garden with every flower that you can wish for, the old gardener cutting the grass of the lawn to the somnolent whirr of the mowing machine, and there compose a stirring sermon against the venial sin of idleness, sipping your glass of cider as you round a well-turned invective against the increase of drinking at the Red Lion or the Glass Bottle. I am sure I should like to be a vicar, if only for ten days, so long as they had two Sundays in them.

I enjoyed that hour in the vicarage garden while I sat upon a deck-chair on the lawn ; I enjoyed it as well as any spent upon that journey. Maytime in a garden is the best of all the year, for a hundred flowers are blooming and all the roses yet to come.

" I don't care," said I to myself as I sat there, " I don't care who says ought to the contrary—it's good to be alive ; and were I the most intellectual pessimist in the world, I would sooner be a brainless optimist if it lost me the pleasure of this day."

I remember a man once saying to me, " Optimism is the last resource of the pessimist."

And as is always the case, when a thing sounds very clever I am at a loss to reply. At a moment like that, it must be something still cleverer, or nothing at all, and in common with most people I am much better when I say nothing at all.

But by the time I had sat down to think about it, I came to the conclusion it was not so clever after all. It was the cry of the pessimist who would be an optimist if he dared, but would never dare for fear of lessening his intelligence in the eyes of others.

I thought of this little epigram that morning as I sat in the vicar's garden. I expect I smiled as I recalled the face of the man who had said it—pale, tired, the face of one who is awake only at night, the hair long and interesting. And from thinking of that, a song came into my head—a flight of fussy sparrows across the lawn no doubt had put it there—

> " 'Twas in the merry month of May,
>   When all the birds were choiring."

What is more, I sang it. There was no one about. I thought I sang it quite well.

XX

THE SPARE BOOTLACE

WE had left Cropredy a little more than an hour, when Eynsham Harry stood still upon the tow-path and pointed across the meadows to where the canal wound under one of the countless bridges.

" Look you, sur," said he, " that bridge on there by the third bend."

I nodded my head.

" 'Tis called old town bridge. I don't know how many years it was ago, but once there was a town there, and a war came what blew it right away. Leastways, that's what they tell me."

I turned and looked at the sloping meadows, spattered with daisies and with cowslips. A score or so of young heifers, white and ruddy brown, were peacefully grazing there ; a few starlings were hovering near them, timid with all their fearlessness to get their food. It seemed impossible to think that a bloody, decimating war could bring about such languid peacefulness as that.

" What was the name of the town ? " I asked.

"I don't know that, sur. I only know there was a town. Sometimes now, I hear, they dig up things in the fields—pots and the like, of what they used to use in the old days. But would you ever think it, sur, to see those fields there? They be filled with larks' nests now."

"'Tis ever the way," said I—"one world builds upon another. How do you know that there are larks' nests there?"

"Look up in the sky, sur."

I looked. Three larks were soaring, infinitely high. Their ceaseless music fell to us like fountain drops of water.

"Their mates are on the nest," said he, "and there be a hundred more of them resting in the grass. 'Tis a fine part of the country this for birds. I've found sedge-warblers, reed-warblers, and black-headed buntings down by the banks of the canal, and there, up in those woods, 'tis full of all sorts."

"Let's come up there now," said I, "and see what we can find. I haven't looked for a nest these eighteen years."

He needed no other word to persuade him, and, tying Fanny to a post by the old town bridge, we set out across the fields in the direction of where the village of Wormleighton with its crown of trees stood high upon the hill surveying all the country round.

On our way to the wood we crossed a country road. Upon a bank of grass by the side of the ditch sat a pedlar eating his lunch, a crust of bread and meat. He was only a pedlar in bootlaces and imitation flowers—conventional roses, red and white, cut out from small turnip heads, the red ones stained with cochineal. A certain craft there was about them, a  certain simplicity which just saved them from the bathos of their foolish wooden stems.

He held them out, and I stopped to look at them. It was then he told me how he cut them out of turnip heads.

" Me own idear, sir—I've never come acrost any as does the likes of 'em. Me own idea hentirely. I've made these for sixty years."

" How old are you now ? " I asked.

" Seventy-three, sir."

" And still tramping the roads ? "

" I don't arst nothin' better, sir."

" And are you always travelling in the same goods ? "

" Well, I varies 'em a bit—studs sometimes, then back to bootlaces, then garters for the girls, then back to studs again."

" But you always sell the roses ? "

" Yes, I find they go—always. 'Tain't no good tellin' a lie about it, but I sold the first of them to the Duchess of Kent, the old Queen's mother."

" I am glad to see you tell the truth about it," said I.

" Well," he replied, " I find it pays."

I walked away.

" There are some tricks," said I to Eynsham Harry, " that are so cheap as can pay no man to work them."

Now, from the moment I had said that, I felt my conscience in reproach against me.

" But I am no fool to be taken in by a ruse of honesty such as that," said I to myself.

" A pedlar must take the world as he finds it," said my Conscience.

" And must pay for his mistakes," said I, " as a tradesman allows for his bad debts."

Now, a Conscience, if you be fool enough to keep one, is a very woman for the last word, to whom, if you would be on your best behaviour, you must stay and listen whether you like it or not.

I thought I had got safe away with that last retort, but the fiend of my Conscience was quick to assure me that had I nothing but a grass bank

on which to sit, a piece of bread and meat for food,
and that begged at a fellow-creature's door, I might
stoop to meaner measures than this pedlar.

I had by this time had enough of it.   The
distance between us was getting greater with every
step, the penalty to pay to my Conscience harder
with every moment.

" If I don't turn back now," said I to myself,
" I shall never do it at all, and make a bed-fellow
of this fiend for the night."   Whereupon, I said
I had suddenly thought of my need of a bootlace,
and, hurrying back, left Eynsham Harry there upon
the road.

" I want a bootlace," said I to the pedlar.

With a ready hand he pulled it out from his
bunch, and what I gave him my Conscience has
more account of than have I.

" 'Tis the ways of one man," said my Conscience,
as I walked back along the road, " 'tis the ways of
one man to tell the truth to keep his pride, while
another tells a lie to save his face."

" 'Tis no lie at all," said I, " for every man on
a journey of this nature must need a bootlace and
to spare."

It was not more than three days later that I had
to fit it into my boot and, calling my Conscience
to account of it, found that she would not answer
me.   Now, isn't that a woman all over ?

XXI

SCHOOL-DAYS

" THERE's one thing," said I, when I had joined
Eynsham Harry again, and we were making our
way across the fields once more to the wood, " there's
one thing where your idea of enjoying yourself falls
short."

" And what's that, sur ? " he asked.

" Spring gone, and you're done for."

" And how's that, sur ? There's more to learn
of a burd than just where she lays her eggs. She
has her young to rear through the early months of
summer ; she has to teach 'en to fly ; she has to
teach 'en the best places where they'd most like find
their food. She has to live herself through the winter.
I've watched the burds here along by the canal ; I've
watched 'en when the snow was four inch deep
along the tow-path, and all these fields were a sheet
of white with never a foot-mark on 'em. And look
you, sur, not that only, but the branches of the trees
and all the hedges with never a leaf on them, white
too, every inch, wherever the snow could settle.

Well, now, sur, if courage is a sort of thing you'd like to think about, you'll see plenty of it then. There's a look in a burd's eye in winter, sur, as I wouldn't care to have to see in any child of mine."

" What sort of a look ? " I asked.

" Well," said he, " 'tis as if the hand of God, as I heard a parson say once, was lifted against 'en. I've known 'en settle on the barge as we went along, so driven was they to look for food. Yes, sur, I think birds is the most couragious creatures there is. Why, do you know, one day a fly-boat came along the five-mile pound between Marston Doles, top of Napton Locks, and Griffin's Bridge at Wormleighton here. She was a steamboat, and was making up for time over the five miles. I suspose a spark must have flown out of her funnel and set fire to a little bush where a thrush was sitting on her young. Anyhow, when I came by, I found the bush all charred and burnt, and all that remained of that poor little burd, still sitting on her nest, burnt to a cinder. She'd never left 'en, not when the flames was all round her. I haven't heard nothin' better'n that, sur, for courage—man or woman."

" Do you know the notes of all the birds ? " I asked presently, for the relation of that little incident would have demanded some moments' silence from anyone. Such a tale you do not hear every day.

" I'm gettin' to know 'en, sur, but it takes me longer'n 'twould most people. I've no more ear for music than my horse, Fanny, has. She knows the crack of a whip, and that's about the only note she'll dance to. I'm little much better myself, and I don't suspose I should ever have taken to study the notes of different burds if hadn't a' been for a gentleman I saw one evening standing on that swing bridge we passed goin' through Thrupp afore we came to Shipton-on-Cherwell. He was standing on the bridge there, and I had to ask 'en to get off so as for the boat to pass through. 'Fine evening,' said he as I came up. I agreed wi' 'en and asked 'en was he looking for fish, for he'd find a sight more of them in the Cherwell. 'There's a pair of reed warblers,' said he, 'built in those rushes last year; I was listening to know if I could hear 'en now.' 'Wouldn't it be better to see 'en?' said I. And then he told me 'ow 'e's sight was so bad he could only just find 'is way about and, being interested in burds, 'e'd learnt all their notes. But then I made out afterwards, sur, that he was an organist in one of these churches you'll find about the country. 'Tis an easy matter for him. I'm getting it meself, but it's a slow job. D'you hear that now?"

We stopped and listened. Amongst all the sounds of birds and insects, I could detect one incessant note. How I knew that that was what he meant, I cannot say; but I was sure of it. It was as when one bids you to listen to a sudden movement in a symphony, and through all the instruments of the orchestra you can detect the notes of one violin, never rising above, but stealing through the harmonious melody of the whole.

" I know that," said I—" it's a chiff-chaff."

He looked at me very steadily for a moment or two.

" If you know more about burds than what I do, sur," said he, " 'twould be kind of you to say so. I've no want to be making a fool of myself before no one."

I laughed.

" You needn't be afraid," said I ; " I used to know them when I was a boy. It's more the school-days coming back again than any knowledge of birds."

Upon this we had plunged into the woods, and, by the time I was half way up my first tree, with Eynsham Harry standing there below me, those days were all come back again. It might have been a half-holiday and I a boy of ten.

XXII

POUR PASSER DOUCEMENT
MA VIE

I REMEMBER, amongst the old china in the Musée Cluny, finding a bowl of that simple design which, you must know, had many years ago belonged to one of simple tastes. It was of green-white china, and upon the inside, in letters of blue that I cannot possibly forget, but could not match were heaven dependent on it, were written the words, *Pour passer doucement ma vie.*

It is often a little thing like that which lives in the memory.

I thought of it again when we reached the little village of Wormleighton. Here indeed is a corner of the world where I could wish gently to pass my life. But I shall say that a hundred times of many another place before this chronicle be ended.

It is the Manor House at Wormleighton where I could wish to spend the rest of my days. A fine piece of Elizabethan architecture it is. Indeed, it may well be older than that. I would not ask that any should rigidly believe me when I talk about architecture.

For the mere trouble of signing one's name in a book, the present owners are magnanimous enough to let one see within. I wondered should I be as generous if it were mine. A stranger seeing over your

house is the pure essence of intrusion. I hate the sight of him, even when I would wish to let and welcome him as a possible tenant.

Yet I felt grateful enough to be shown over the Manor House at Wormleighton. In September of 1571 the Earl of Leicester with a brilliant retinue stayed there on his way to meet Queen Elizabeth at Warwick. She too, upon her progress from Edgecote to Warwick by way of Long Itchington, she too slept the night there ere she passed on to meet her Leicester.

But it is the memories of Prince Rupert which cling closest to the place. There you may still see the Star Chamber where he dined the night before the battle of Edgehill.

"There is one panelled room," said the little maid who showed me round. "Would you like to see that?"

I said that indeed I would, and straightway she took me there.

Before we entered, she knocked softly on the old oak door. A voice as softly from within bid us enter. The little maid opened the door, and there, in no large room, but panelled to the ceiling in warm, brown oak, sat an old lady by the mullioned window, a sewing basket upon her lap and in her hands a piece of embroidery through which her needle glittered and disappeared, glittered and disappeared to every movement of her skilful fingers.

Never in my life have I felt such an intruder as I did then.

She bowed to me and I bowed to her.

"It's very beautiful," I muttered foolishly.

"It is indeed," said she, and fell to working at her embroidery again, never dreaming that I had meant not only the panelling; never dreaming that in that word beautiful I had included the glimpse of the old garden outside, and above all herself. Indeed the

Thames and Severn Canal.　Maintenance work at the west end of Sapperton Tunnel

Thames and Severn Canal. 'Old Willum' the lengthman, near Latton

panelling was wonderful, the garden was wonderful too.   But it was she who made the picture.   I shall remember her when all these other things have gone out of my head.

In another moment I had thanked her, excused myself and retired.   And as I walked down the passages into the garden once more, those words on the old bowl in the Musée Cluny came softly back into my mind—" *Pour passer doucement ma vie.*"

XXIII

THE HEDGEROW PHILOSOPHY

Soon after Wormleighton, we passed the last of those Oxfordshire bridges which make so characteristic a feature in all that meadow landscape. Onwards from there, through Marston Doles and Napton, it was scarce worth one's while to travel.

I sat disconsolately on the cabin roof and hoped for better things, but they did not come. We passed no village of interest then. It seemed as though the canal had wilfully sought deserted channels. For the first few corners that we reached, every hope I had rose expectant at the thought of what might be beyond. That is the best of a corner in this world. At least it promises; without which, hope might die of sheer starvation. Even a promise, broken, is something to live upon; yet there comes a time when they are but husks in the mouth. I grew tired of these broken promises at last.

" Does it improve at all between this and Coventry ? " I asked Eynsham Harry presently.

He looked at me steadily, and then—which is an event with him—he smiled.

" It's very samesome, sur," said he, " all the ways from here to Coventry."

" Then why did you smile ? " I asked.

" Well, sur," he replied, " if you'll pardon me saying so, there be nothing the matter wi' you, but that you be young."

" You mean foolish ? " said I, for it would seem that one has to be well-advanced in years before one makes a compliment out of the accusation of youth.

" No, sur, I said nothing so impertinent. 'Twas young I said, and young I means. You want your cake before you've eat your bread and butter. 'Tis the way wi' my son John—' If you're not hungry enough,' I say to 'en, ' to eat your bread and butter first, you ain't hungry enough to eat cake.' "

" I've heard that argument before, you know," said I. " It rakes up memories of days I'd give much to live over again. But it's not sound. It never convinced me then. It doesn't even convince me now. I've stodged myself many a time to get to my piece of cake. It only takes the gilt off the gingerbread by the time you do come to it.'

" Well—isn't that a good thing, sur ? " said he. " The cake is not so wholesome, and it costs more than bread and butter. Come a time and you'll do without it altogether."

It is not that I am accustomed to having the better of an argument; but I felt none the less surprised that I came off so badly in this.

"Now where do you," said I, "who neither know how to read nor write—where do you get your logic from?"

"I don't know, sur," he replied—and with such honesty as I would give much to meet with every day—"I don't know, sur, for I don't rightly understand 'ee when 'ee talks about logic. I says what I thinks, and mostly I thinks what I finds. This world ain't no easier to live in, sur, for the help of luxuries. There's scarce a man finds an easier place of the world than that tramp we met selling bootlaces outside Wormleighton. They say the more you have the more you want, but, by God! it's the more you have, the less you can do without. Now, that ain't making the world an easy place to live in."

"Then why?" said I, "did you refuse my offer of twenty shillings a week and look for thirty?"

When a man is talking as much sense as this, it is taking no mean advantage to put such a question to him. He took it quite good-naturedly. He smiled as he thought of our bargain in the Nag's Head.

"Because," said he, "the more you have, sur, the more you want, and the more you want, the more you have to pay for it. When a gentleman like you comes out a-boating for little more than a holiday and offers five shillings more a week than a man expects, 'tis only right to take it that he's offered less than he's ready to pay."

"Good Lord!" I exclaimed, "d'you mean to say that fifteen shillings would have been enough?"

"It would indeed, sur—and I'll take it now, if so be you think I've not done fairly by you."

I lay back on the cabin roof, and, upon my soul, I laughed.

"You're quite right," said I. "One does these things so often with one's eyes open, that after a time they become glazed. I remember once when I lived near Covent Garden, I used to get up early of a morning before the market closed, and I'd get Darwin tulips for twopence a bunch. Now, when I go to a florist up west, they charge me a shilling. What's more, I pay it. It's the same thing."

"Well, I'll take fifteen shillings, sur," he repeated, "if so be you think I haven't done fairly by you."

"I'd sooner give you five more than fifteen less," said I. "A man's philosophy is worth it any day of the week. But what I want to know is, where you learn these things. You say you think what you find; but what do you find?"

He was silent for a moment while he took the narrow passage beneath a bridge. When we had

come out into the open canal once more, he turned
and looked at me.

"Well, sur, last year I was coming along this
very pound, and as I came by a corner down there—
I was just in front of Fanny on the tow-path—I
started up a hawk from the hedge. I thought she
could be up to no good, so I marked the place with
me eye, and at first when I came along I could see
nothing. But when I went down on me hands and
knees, I made out a dead field-mouse—them little
creatures wi' the pointy nose, the size of a man's little
finger. Did I say she was dead ? She wasn't quite.
The little beast was quivering. The hawk had dug
her out of her hole, and there was the little store of
nuts and berries she'd set by her for the winter time,
all scattered about in the grass.

"'Look you here, mother,' I said to my wife.
'Whenever you've got a sixpence in your pocket
and want to buy something you don't need, just make
a little nest of it.'

"'If you mean that mouse,' said she, 'what's the
good when the hawk came and took it ?'"

I echoed that good lady's sentiments to the letter.

"Had I seen that," said I, "it would have driven
me to the utmost limits of extravagance."

"Well, 'tis curious," said Eynsham Harry, "the
way people do argue. If it hadn't been for that
kestrel, I might never have learnt that 'tis the ways
of the field-mouse to make her store for the winter

months. The first thing I reckoned was that for one mouse that had been killed, there were a thousand what had made their store against winter in safety. Why, there must be hawks, sur, and hawks must live, same as Jews and company promoters, but it isn't every man as need be caught by 'em."

"It comes to this," said I, "that you're the true-

born philosopher. You learn your philosophy from the hedgerows. I only play at it."

"Well, sur," said he, "I've often sat and looked into a hedge where all the insects be creepin', and I've said to myself : 'You be near as ever you be in your life to the greatest secret in the world.' But, bi God, I've never found it, sur."

I turned away, disheartened with my own shortcomings.

"Where does that branch of the canal lead to ?" I asked presently. We were approaching a bridge on the right, raked over the water in a long low curve that made a picture in itself.

"That, sur," said he, "is the branch of the Warwick and Napton."

"It goes right into the town?"

"Yes, sur."

"Then let's turn out of this," said I, "and stop the night at Warwick."

XXIV

WARWICK

When I saw the countless volumes showing in the windows of the booksellers, all relating to Warwick and its environs, I said, "Not one word of the history of Warwick will I write. This voyage of the *Flower of Gloster* is a voyage of discovery. I can find nothing here but what has been found already."

Yet what one can say of Warwick beside the relation of its history, it puzzles me to know. I was debating on that very subject as I walked up the High Street, my attention first this way and then that, yet history, nothing but the history of England, stared me in the face. Outside Leicester's hospital, a man was acting guide to a group of people, and to every word he said, their mouths, almost imperceptibly, widened in aperture.

"It's no good telling us all those names," I heard one of them say at last—" we shan't remember one of 'em. Just let's know when it was built and if those beams are real oak. We've got to go over the Castle yet, and by schedule we must catch the late train to Stratford-on-Avon."

I stood for a moment to listen, and in five minutes heard the history of Leicester's hospital over three hundred and fifty odd years. When he had finished, the speaker of the group turned to one of his companions.

"Did the Morgans see this place when they were in Warwick?" he asked.

"No," said the other. He shook his head to emphasise it.

"Well," said the first, "we can tell 'em all about it. Three hundred and fifty years—it's great."

I walked on, trying to think of those three hundred and fifty years. It was impossible. I could only think of that five minutes.

A few yards down the street, a man stopped, smiled genially, and thrust out a hand of welcome.

"Hallo, Matherson!" he exclaimed jovially, "never thought I should find you in Warwick."

"No more of a surprise, Cubberwheat," said I at a venture, "than my finding you here."

Now, I never saw anything quite so sudden as the fall of that man's expression. In one moment it dropped the full ninety degrees which lie between pleasant satisfaction and offended dignity. Matherson, no doubt, was a man whom he wished to stand well with; Matherson was a man whom he was proud to know.

" My name's not Cubberwheat ! " said he emphatically, with insult ringing in his voice.

" My name's not Matherson," said I.

" What ! not Matherson of Coventry ? " he asked, for if I were not Matherson of Kamschatka, he was determined to have it that I was Matherson of somewhere.

" Not even Matherson of Coventry," said I.

" Well—I'm certainly not Cubberwheat," said he. " Cubberwheat ! " he added in disdain, and thereat turned upon his heel abruptly leaving me to stand in the street.

Apart from a slightly wanting sense of humour, I have nothing to say against this gentleman's pride. Doubtless his name was Jones ; but whatever it was, to anyone save Cubberwheat himself, the name Cubberwheat is an insult.   But it is quite amusing when you think that it applies also to the name of Jones. If I were to address Mrs Cubberwheat—supposing she exists—by the name of Jones, I doubt if a sense of humour would save her.   It would be a great one if it did.

Seemingly, not only is the Englishman's home his castle, but his name is the flag he flies to show he is in residence.

I took a furnished house in the country once, and the owner assured me, with a marked tone of seriousness in his voice, that there was a flag-staff in the garden and a Union Jack in the boot-cupboard under the stairs.

" Of course, if you have to go up to town,"
said he, " you can just put the flag back into the
cupboard."

" Then why is the rent only three guineas a
week ? " I asked him.

He shook his head sorrowfully, for I had signed
the agreement by then.

" It ought to be more," said he.

" Undoubtedly, it ought," said I.

" But I hear you write books," he added.

I admitted the impeachment.

" Well, if you like," said he, " you can put the
place into your next book.   You can use the address.
I don't mind."

" Some of my books have a very bad name,"
I warned him.

" Oh ! then perhaps you'd better leave it alone,"
said he.   " At anyrate, here's the key of the boot-
cupboard."

I wish that more people had his sense of humour
and that less were conscious of what they have.

I passed another bookshop after I had left my
friend Cubberwheat.   Within the window I saw
volumes bearing the titles, " Shakespeare's Land,"
" Warwick and its History," " Shakespeare's Avon,"
and so on.

" I'm sure there will be nothing about Warwick
in my barge book," I said to myself.   And there
is not.

XXV

THE GATE INTO THE BLACK COUNTRY

I HAD been into the Black Country before. I had driven over many of those roads through the charred heart of that desert of land, which is more like to death than the Dead Sea. It is an awful yet wonderful part of the world. God has deserted it—left it absolutely to the hand of man. And in those hands, as one might well suppose, all but human nature lies dead. All the green goodness of the earth has gone. From one mile to another there is no blade of grass will live. The very mould is black, a bed of ashes in which not even a weed could find its nourishment.

I have heard the complaint, half jest, half earnest, that the Almighty might have done things better than He has. " If I were God," a modern author titled some pamphlet that he wrote. That, no doubt, was the jest in earnest. But you have only to go into the Black Country to know what can be done with a wonderful world when God delivers it into the hand of man.

I know very well that there, is the pulse of England's greatness, that out of Bradford, Halifax, Huddersfield, Rochdale and Burnley, the stream of molten metal flows through the veins and arteries of a great nation, nerves her to face her enemies, and feeds those energies by which alone she can maintain her position in the world.

But what a price to pay, and what a coinage to pay it in !   If you believe in the efficacy of war, then doubtless the Black Country will seem most wonderful to your mind.   In fact, whether you believe in it or not, those belching furnaces and that poisoned land must make you marvel as you pass it by.   The black sweeping hills with scrubby bushes leafless and dead ; the men and women, white-faced and dirty with the everlasting falling of the sooty air ; the thousand factories and the countless furnaces ; the utter lifelessness in all this seething mass of life, however much he might shudder at it, a man must stop and realise its greatness.

There are two places in the world which seem like hell to me, two places which, if I had the making of hell, I would closely imitate ; the one is Monte Carlo and the other the Black Country, two opposite poles, the last extremes of luxury and labour.

And here, all the year round, thousands and thousands of human beings work out their salvation. One almost asks if salvation be possible ; for not only the skin but the lungs, not only they but the heart, and not only the heart but the very soul of a people

must be blackened in such an atmosphere. It seems fitting in irony, that when they take their holidays, they should throng to a place called Blackpool—a very pandemonium of amusements where for a time they can forget the sweat and labour of their daily lives.   It is just forgetting, and that is all.

Now Birmingham, beside being the centre of all the canal traffic of England, is, as it were, the outer gate of all this sunless country.   Why I should have gone so far as even to approach it again, I can scarcely understand.

"If it's the country you want to see, sur," Eynsham Harry warned me, "then have my advice and do nothing wi' Birningame.   I've seen more dead dogs and cats in the water between Knowle and Olton Bridge than ever I have thrushes in the hedges."

Notwithstanding even this, I went, and to this moment regret the hours we wasted.   From Turner's Green to Knowle, along a ten-mile pound, the surrounding country might well be worse.   Then came the six locks at Knowle, up which we climbed wearily, a height, it must have been, of over a hundred feet before we reached the top.   The only one of us who really enjoyed it was Fanny.   Here she was given the bucket with her fodder, and for the next hour, while we raised and lowered one lock after another, munched steadily with that appetising sound all horses make when they are eating.

At the end of it, I caught a glance from Eynsham Harry as I stood up to ease my back ; there was, as well, the suspicion of a smile in his eye.

"What is it ? " I asked.

"Do you think you'd like the life a-boatin', sur ? " he inquired solemnly.

"Life is much the same whichever way you take it," said I. "I've never met a road yet but what it had a hill to it some way or other."

"Quite true, sur," said he; "and it isn't even experience will teach some people what they can expect to find on the other side of the hill before they sets to climb it."

Then I understood the light of laughter in his eye.

"You mean we've sweated up these six locks for nothing?" said I.

"Well, sur, there's no sweating, if he comes by it honest, can hurt any man; but you don't be the gentleman wi' the tastes I think you have, if you like your journey on from Knowle to Birningame."

No one ever assessed my tastes so accurately. I chafed against it the whole journey; but when a man has put himself in the way of a bad bargain, he is not going readily to admit he is made a fool of. I stuck to my pride as long as I could; sat on my favourite seat on the cabin roof, and hailed with joy a bank of blue-bells which lent their colour in a deep purple to the dark reflection of the dirty water.

Eynsham Harry said nothing, but I felt that he was just biding his time till we should come to the outskirts of Birmingham. And after Solihull, they began in earnest. The ugly buildings of the labourers and artisans commenced to line the canal side. The trees and fields grew less and less in number. He had not exaggerated for a moment, when he spoke

o the dead dogs and cats in the water.   One after
another we passed them, their milk-white swollen
bodies lifting high above the stagnant water.

Even the men passing us through the locks lay
inert and lifeless on their cabin roofs, as though the
journey of the last few days through all that blackened
country had brought them to exhaustion.

At last I turned to Eynsham Harry and admitted
my folly.

" You're quite right," said I : " there are some
hills it would be as well to learn of before one climbs
them.   What's the quickest way out of this ? "

He never so much as showed a sign of triumph
when I admitted my defeat.

"Our best way now, sur," said he, "would be to turn back till we come to Lapworth. There be a junction there wi' the Stratford-on-Avon canal going through Preston Bagot and Wootton-Wawen. I think maybe that 'ud more suit your fancy. 'Tis

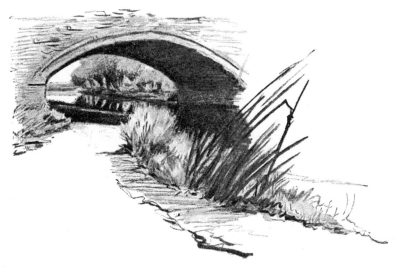

close by Henley-in-Arden, and the world's quieter there'n what it be here."

I swung the tiller over straight away as he un-hitched the tow-line.

"May I never realise again," said I, "how great a country England is."

And there are many who, if they stood at the outer gate of the Black Country, would say the same.

XXVI

THE STRATFORD-ON-AVON
CANAL

I NEVER did a better piece of business than when I took Eynsham Harry's advice and turned back to Lapworth. To be quite accurate, the junction of the two canals is at Kingswood, and from there through Preston Bagot is but a matter of thirteen miles. But the waterway, as I passed along it in the *Flower of Gloster*, was deserted, and they are thirteen miles right out of the track of the world.

Sometimes, they tell me, a barge makes its solitary way down to Stratford, but the locks have in the crevices of their gates all that luxuriant growth of water-weed which shows you how seldom they are used.

Many and many a mile of canal in England now is thrown out of service by the iron roads, which as yet have not succeeded—as also the canals, to the critical eye of Anna Lætitia—in fitting themselves into the landscape. Will they ever indeed become so intimate a part of the soil as have the harrow and the plough ? Truly, I wonder what Anna Lætitia would have to say, did she hear the thunder of the express down one of the great railroads through this very country she loved so well ? Quite easily could I imagine her now sitting down at her desk to write another paper, but this time in praise of the Stratford-on-Avon canal ; calling forth the evil Genius of that iron road which has drawn its fretted lines across the face of Nature, thrilling her reader thereby with the horrors of civilisation. And if in those days she abused the canal, what would she say of the Black Country now ? Certainly she would no longer put on her white cambric and her black gloves. I can see her in crape and jet from top to toe.

But now from the dull crape of the Black Country we came to the meadows once more, all in their spring muslin, and such muslin as only Nature knows the weaving of. The white thorn hedges were half in bloom, the buds some green, some breaking white. That alone is a trimming of lace which the most cunning fingers in Spain have never equalled, not even for a prince's cradle or a cardinal's robe. Here and again in the hedgerows stood a crab-apple tree, pink-white in bloom. Did they ever in France paint such dainty flowers on silk as these? And by the water's edge grew those reeds, yet young enough to keep their pale flesh-

colour before they swelled into the full green of summer.

What a joy it was after the smoke and ashes of Birmingham! I lay full stretched upon the cabin roof, my face in my hands, the sun beating down upon my head, drinking it in as, in summer, the labourer in the corn-fields drinks his jug of cider to ease the parched dryness of his throat.

" How can a man care for that devastating march of civilisation," said I, " when it means the ultimate destruction of such places in the world as this ? God knows we must progress ; we cannot stop still. The mind must grow, or it will atrophy.   But if ever a plant needed light in which to bear its flower, that plant is the mind."

But this is just the way a man talks when God is in His Heaven and the complete rightness of the world is on every side of him.   It is, as a matter of fact, only in the deepest tribulation of his soul that he speaks truth ; for when everything goes well with him a man has little judgment to boast about, and says the first thing which, with the lightness of a feather, rises flamboyant to his head.

I could not have found such great wisdom in what I said aloud that morning as I lay stretched out on the cabin roof of the *Flower of Gloster*, because, no sooner had I said it than I began to sing—with such voice as God has given me—all the snatches of songs, every one I knew.   Where I had forgotten the words, I made them up.   Sometimes they rhymed, sometimes they did not.   It was a happy matter of chance.

" 'Twas in the merry month of May
   When all the birds were choiring."

I began with that, no doubt because it was still
in my head from that morning in Cropredy. In
the country, a tune such as this stays with you
an unconscionable length of time. You hum it to
yourself last thing at night before you go to sleep ;
you wake up, and there it is still with you in the
morning.

Now, all this is better than any philosophy. A
man who can sing to himself—when, in such a case
as mine, it cannot be particularly pleasant for him to
listen to—is far on the way towards taking life in
the easiest way imaginable.

It is surely not all a question of mating when
birds raise their voices ? What mistress can ever
hear her master, the lark, when he sings up in those
heights of air in the dim distant chancel of the clouds ?
I am quite certain that even Bellwattle, whose
only knowledge of music is composed of a couple
of lines from the most antiquated ballads that
were ever composed in the early fifties, would
never have listened to me that morning for five
minutes.

No ; when a man sings to himself, it is because
he can dispense with all philosophy. Wherefore,
I did away with my speculations upon the progress
of the mind. It mattered little to me then whether,

like a bulb, it could grow in darkness, or, like a seed, it must have the light. All that mattered was the whole world, decked in muslin; and so I sang, with what effect I have already given you to suppose.

XXVII

LOWSON FORD

In those parts they call it Lonesome Ford. That is better than just the giving it of a good name. 'Tis as

though from long association the place had named itself. It lies alone in a cup of the hills like a polished pebble in the deep pool of a twinkling brook. Right through the centre of the village runs the canal under an old red-stone bridge, with the low tiled lock-house just beside it. Here and there the old half-timbered cottages are placed with but little sense of order—rough facets of the stone that glitter with colour as you look down on the village from the hills above.

There may be other villages in England more peaceful than this, but in my journey in the *Flower of Gloster* I never came across them. In towns and cities the houses can well be said to be awake. There is an alertness about the appearance of their windows ; the doors open and shut with a sound that has life even in its echo. But here in Lowson Ford all men and things would seem to be asleep. The cottage windows open to the sun, the doors ajar, the gardens patient in the heat ; even the farmers' wag-gons, with their heavy wheels and cumbrous horses, saunter through the street all as in the idle causeless-ness of slumber.

I would not for one moment say they do not work in Lowson Ford. I saw farm labourers coming and going from the White Horse Inn, so work there must have been a-doing somewhere. But had they been going and coming from the White Horse Inn in their hundreds, then I should only have felt that it was I who was asleep, dreaming one of those mad summer dreams when things happen, all dis-proportionate to what they are.

You could well spend a summer in the village of
Lowson Ford and forget that the world was moving
round about you.   It   is   an   event,   unparalleled

almost in excitement, when a barge comes through
to Stratford.   Then all the little boys and girls rush
down the street to the old red-stone bridge to watch

it as it passes through the lock. The fat lock-keeper's wife wakes from her long months of som-nolence, bestirs herself under the admiring eye of all the children, though she has nothing whatever to do. Her big woolly dog, of such a breed as I have never seen before or since, rouses himself from the sun-warmed coping stones of the lock and follows after her, with a sense of importance, half awake, watching her with his eyes wherever she goes. Oh, Lowson Ford, I can tell you, is wide awake then, when a barge goes through the lock ! But the barge goes on its way into the busy world ; the smoke of its little chimney from the cabin fire trails round the corner and, blue as it is, melts into the bluer air of distance. Then Lowson Ford turns on its side once more, and for many a month to come sleeps like a baby in its cradle of the hills. If ever I need sleep to wake again, I shall go and find my pillow there.

Yet even in such a place as this, so grim a thing as tragedy can find its way. But then, as you might so well suppose, it is not the tragedy of distorted face, of twisted features of the like you find in cities. The little tragedy I met in Lowson Ford had not such ugliness as made me shudder when I came face to face with it.

It was making late in the afternoon when we came there. There was that warmer colour in the sun as when it throws its light through the dust and heat of the day's journey. The whole village seemed deserted, though through the open doors of the cottages I could just make out the old women seated over their evening meal, pouring the tea from warm brown earthenware tea-pots into their big kitchen cups, nodding their heads and gossiping.   Old women must talk, for Nature leaves them little else to do.

But one figure commanded all my interest, even my curiosity.   He stood on the bridge looking down the canal at the *Flower of Gloster*, watching her silently as she entered the lock, crossing to the other side, still watching us in silence as we came through into the open pound once more.

Here we moored her to the canal bank and, jumping off, I came up on to the bridge to speak with him.   He had that look of a man who has yielded up all his active interest in a busy world and is content to be a silent spectator of the life which passes close around him.

"If of nothing else," thought I, "I shall learn something of Lowson Ford."

He looked just the sort of man who would be proud of being the oldest inhabitant.   Yet he was not so old, after all.

"Thirty years I've been here, sir," said he.

"And what age are you now ? " I asked.

"Seventy-one."

"You get the pension, then ? "

"Well "—he smiled—" I'm qualified for it, as age goes.   But I've a little bit of land and a cottage

of my own.   I don't take the pension.   I'm quite comfortable—as comfortable as I shall ever wish to be."

He pointed to a little half-timbered cottage, just climbing up the hill.   I could see the late tulips like brilliant coloured stones in the prim mosaic of the garden's flowers.

"'Tis a charming place," said I.   "If I were your age, I would not ask better than to spend the rest of my days there."

His eyes looked very firmly out before him, and under his white beard and moustache I saw his lips set as though he were suffering a pain he would have no one know of.

"May be I'll stay there," said he slowly—"I haven't made up my mind."

"You don't mean to say you're going to move?"

He just bent his head in the affirmative.

"But not into a town?" I asked.

"No, sir—no—not into a town.   I lived in London once, when first I married—but—but it didn't agree with—my wife.   We moved then to Basingstoke—that didn't agree with her either. Then we came here, and we've been here thirty years."

"How long have you been married?"

"Fifty-one years."

His eyes blinked quickly and he screwed his lips again.   I had almost asked him what pain it was, when the look passed away once more and silence came beside us for a while.

"Is your wife up at the cottage?" I asked presently.

He nodded his head, but never turned his eyes to look in that direction. And then I felt impelled to notice something strange. It was more than the look that had passed across his face. It was more than the pain I thought he had spasmodically been suffering. His eyes were filled with water ; but that I imagined might well be the weakness of old age. The whites of them were tinged with red. But as the strangeness of his manner impressed me, I began to think I had not read these signs aright. Suddenly I felt awkward, ill at ease. It came upon me quickly that he wished to be alone. Whereupon I asked him if he had had his tea, thinking doubtless of those passing glimpses I had got through the cottage doors as we came by.

He shook his head.

"Well—you mustn't let me keep you," said I. "I expect tea is your best meal in the day."

Then he turned his face and looked at me, and never have I seen so deep a look of suffering in the face of any man. It seemed as if he knew more agony of mind than he could bear.

"I've been trying to go this last hour," he muttered brokenly, "but I daren't."

"Daren't? Why not?"

"My wife died yesterday—sir—she's—lying up there in the cottage."

Once more came silence to ease us. He leant back again on the bridge, and the muscles in his face were twitching under the thin white hairs of his beard.

There is nothing ugly in such a tragedy as this ; but it is none the less great for that. I thought of the utter desolation in his mind ; for many a time, no doubt, he had stood upon that bridge, watching the life of the village until the welcome hour came that called him up to tea. And now, of all the hours in his day of desolation, this was the most terrible he must face.

"I'm sorry," I said lamely—" I'm sorry I did not understand sooner."

He shut his lips as he made another effort to be brave.

"That's all right, sir. I tried to tell you before, but it was difficult. It is a great parting, you know, after fifty-one years."

I have remembered that simple phrase of his best of all—" It is a great parting." How great a parting it must be, I do not dare to think ; for after such a time neither a man nor a woman run their race alone, but like little children, confidingly, hand in hand.

A few words more to make our parting less abrupt, and then I thought it best to leave him. One fights these tragedies best alone.

I walked through the village then and came eventually to the barge by another way. Fanny was hitched once more to the tow-line, and we set off. As we turned the corner of the hill, I looked back. He was still there, still resting both his arms upon the bridge. He had not dared as yet to go back to his tea. What is more, I knew he never would. The late evening must creep down the village street, and then, when the shadows spread their cloaks over the things one sees so plainly in the day, he would steal back alone to his cottage and with wide eyes watch through the night until 'twas day once more.

XXVIII

YARNINGDALE FARM

Steep, on one side the canal, between Lowson Ford
and Preston Bagot, the high land continues for a mile
or so, and, soon after we had turned the corner, leaving the village out of sight, I took to the tow-path,
walking for a while there alone by Fanny's side.

That old fellow on the bridge had brought me
the need of silence and my own company.   Even the
philosophy of Eynsham Harry would have seemed
out of place, though I have no doubt he would have
had much to say that was wise upon the matter.
One may not think conclusively by oneself—I am
sure that I do not,—but at least one thinks pleasantly.
Even that tragedy, as I thought over it alone, seemed
to fill me with a sense of awe which I could not call
unpleasant.   I should only have found its irony had
I talked of it aloud.

So I walked alone with Fanny, soothed, I have
no doubt of it, by the unvarying expression of her
face as she toiled monotonously along the tow-path.
Often I glanced at her, and she suggested nothing

to alter the even tenor of my mind. Those were peaceful days, those days on the *Flower of Gloster*.

" Sur ! "

I looked back.

" Will 'ee take the tiller a while and let me get back ? Look you, I forgot to get milk in Lonesome Ford. The jug's empty."

It seemed a pity that he should have all the way to go back. I looked about me right and left. On the crest of the hill above us there was a house in the midst of a clump of elms. Apple trees blossomed near it. I could see their white lime-washed trunks. There were outhouses beside. Assuredly it was a farm.

" I'll climb up there," said I. " Give me the jug. That's a farm. They're bound to have some there."

He handed it to me over the side, and, taking a gap in the hedge, I set off up the steep grass slope, still glad to be alone.

They had made the hill an orchard, and never do fruit trees offer so fine a pageant of their blossoms as when, tier upon tier, they rise above each other up a steep hill-side. And here, on the crown of the hill, in the midst of its orchard of white-trunked apple-trees spread with bloom, stood an old English farm-house, one of those places that seem to make English history a thing of yesterday. If I came across one, I came across a thousand in that journey in the *Flower of Gloster*, and each fresh place I found had all the new wonder of age to make it as beautiful as the last.

Through a wooden gate into a small odd garden before the house—where flowers grew, it would seem, more by favour because they liked the place than from any care or cultivation,—I found a path of uneven flag-stones up to the door. There I knocked, waited, and then knocked again. There was no answer.

In the farm-yard close by, the chickens were scratching in the hay ; an old cow chewed the cud under the apple-trees in the orchard. She had a rolling jaw and a calm eye, which she quietly fixed on me. As good as speaking, she told me that no one was at home. On the window-sill outside an open latticed window a black cat lay fast asleep, where the last light of the day's sun could warm her. A brood of young chickens peeped out of the bars of their coop as I still waited on the step before the door. Yet I could not believe that the place was utterly deserted. The farmer's wife would come presently. She was out at the back of the house doing her share in the work of the farm. But no—I heard no one. I looked up at the bedroom windows : they were all closed. Then, just as I was about to knock again, I realised that the open window was to my purpose.

As I stepped across to it, the black cat opened her eyes, stretched forth her front paws and yawned. Her mouth and tongue were scarlet. A tulip in the bed below her was not a brighter red. But she moved no more than this, even when I leant across her and peeped into the room through the open window.

For a moment, in the strong contrast of the shade with the sunlight outside, I could see nothing. By degrees it grew more plain. It was their parlour into which I looked. There was the old open chimney with the broad oak beam above it. The beams across the ceiling were black with age. A big bowl of cowslips stood on the table, covered with brown, shining oil-cloth in the middle of the room ; and on a Victorian horse-hair sofa against the further wall, there lay an old woman, the oldest woman I think I have ever seen in my life. She must have been near a hundred years old. Her face was so wrinkled and her skin so shrunken and white that it seemed, had you pricked her cheek, no blood could possibly have come. She was asleep. My knocking had not wakened her. I crept back to the door, lifted the latch, and entered.

She *was* asleep. I crossed over on tip-toe to her side, and for a moment stood there, listening. Her breathing was like the faint stirring of leaves in the willow trees by the side of water on a day in summer when nothing but a willow leaf is fine enough to tell you of the wind. But it was even and regular. An old clock upon the wall ticked just twice as fast as came her breathing. I counted it.

It was only for a moment I thought of waking

her.   It was more I thought I could not than I could.
Then I crept out of the room into the back part of
the house, thinking surely that there I should find the
farmer's wife.   Again, no !   My search was not fruit-
less, however, for in the kitchen there was a cradle
standing some few feet from the fire—quite safe,—
and in the cradle there lay asleep a minute little
baby.   To my unpractised eye, it might have just
been born.   For as the old lady in the parlour
seemed to me the oldest person I had ever seen in
my life, so this infant appeared to me the youngest.
And these two, sleeping there in absolute peacefulness, were the sole guardians of the security of Yarn-
ingdale Farm.   I found no one else—not a soul.

So then I crept out of the kitchen, my heart
in my mouth lest I should waken them, and, con-
tinuing my progress of discovery, found at last the
dairy.   There, on cool dark slabs of slate, were five
large shallow cans, full of milk.   Choosing the one
on which the cream had scarcely settled—for when
one is a thief one can still ape the gentleman,—
filled my jug and crept back again into the parlour.
There on the table, beside the bowl of cowslips, I put
some money, and taking a little piece of paper from
my pocket I wrote : " I have taken a pint of your
milk from the dairy without disturbing either of
your babies."

Only I wrote it in printed letters, because they
tell me my writing is vile.

XXIX

THE COMPLEAT ANGLER

I CALLED him compleat because, had he not been a fisherman, both life for him and he for life would have been the most pitifully insufficient.

We saw him in the distance as we came towards Preston Bagot, and, from the strained motionlessness of his attitude, I got it into my head he was at that crucial moment in a fisherman's day—not when he has a bite, but when he thinks he has. So I ran down the plank to the tow-line mast and pulled the rope. Fanny was only too ready to stop. I would not have disturbed him in that moment for the world.

But it was a false alarm, as I soon found out when I descended to the tow-path and had come up quietly to his side. This attitude of tensity he maintained the whole time while I stood and watched him.

"Any luck?" I asked presently, which is the proper and conventional thing to inquire of your fisherman, showing, as it does, a lively interest, without casting any slight upon his skill.

He shook his head, but never looked up at me, never took his eyes from off that red-and-white float, depending motionless in the water from the end of his line.

"How long have you been here?"

"Since breakfast."

"And caught nothing?"

He shook his head again.

"P'raps you've got a bad place?"

"None of it good round here," said he. But I detected no note of regret in his voice; he did not say it in the tone of one who yearns for what he has not.

"Then why not give it up? said I; "you're only wasting your time."

" Nothing else to do," he replied.

" Why, are you taking a holiday ? "

" All holidays now," said he.

" How's that ? "

" Little while back," said he casually, " I fell forty feet."

Fell forty feet ! My heavens, but he was proud of it ! That casual voice, that abrupt announcement, were both indicative of his pride. He was like the pedlar I met outside Wormleighton. He did not wish to tell a lie about it. He would never have informed me it was thirty-nine feet. That would not have been true. No, it was forty feet, and there he was to tell the story.

" I was laid up six months," he continued presently—" twelve operations. I've got a silver plate in my head—two fractures in my right arm, one in my left. One leg's cut off below the knee, and I had three ribs broken. Forty feet's a good tidy distance, you know. You can't fall forty feet without having something to show for it."

" But do you mean to say," said I, " that that's all the damage you received ? "

There is a certain sweetness in the pleasure of taking down a man's pride even when he has gone so far as to fall forty feet to arrive at it.

" You fell forty feet ! " I continued mercilessly, " and that's all that happened to you ! "

Then he did look round at me and with such an

expression of injured dignity as multiplied my simple pleasure a thousand times.

" Ain't that enough ? " said he, " a compound and a simple fracture, an amputation, a silver plate, twelve operations ?   Why, one of the nurses said to me I was as good as a full hospital to a medical student.   Well, I know the biggest I ever heard of a man falling and still being alive was twenty-three feet. I had it sent me—a cutting out of a paper.   I fell forty."

" Did you measure it ? " I asked.

" No, but a pal of mine did.   It was off of a scaffold.   When he saw I was alive, he went and measured it afterwards."

It was then I saw how, not only had he achieved greatness, but that greatness had been thrust upon him.

" It must have made you a lot of friends," said I.

He turned back his eyes to his float.

" At any rate, they think more of it than what you seem to," said he.

" Oh, I think it's a fine performance," I replied ; " but I must say, if I'd fallen forty feet——"

" Do you think you'd have more to show for it than what I have ? "

" Well, for two days subsequent," said I, " I think I should ; after that I hope they'd bury me— as decently as the circumstances permitted."

" Oh, yes—you mean it 'ud have killed you," he added triumphantly.   Then he looked round again and sized me up and down. "And I expect it would," said he; "but you see I got over it. I can come here and fish. I can't work, but I can come here and fish."

"Well, it's mainly a matter of taste," said I. "If ever I fall forty feet—and I think twenty would be quite enough for me,—we shall find that our tastes differ. It's only right that they should. The world would be a damnably uninteresting place if every man who fell forty feet preferred that it should kill him outright rather than leave him with a single capacity for fishing."

He took his line slowly out of the water, and very thoughtfully—if, indeed, with a silver plate in his head one is capable of any thought—he put more bait on the hook. He had probably had it in the water since mid-day without any at all.

I was about to turn away then and go back to the barge, when a notice-board on the other side of the hedge caught my eye.

"Notice.—All persons fishing in this water without proper leave will be prosecuted.

£1 Reward

will be paid to anyone giving information that shall lead to a conviction.

"W. Shakespeare,
"Preston Bagot."

"Is this gentleman any relation?" I asked.

He looked over his shoulder.

" Of mine ? " said he.

" No," said I, " of one they used to call William Shakespeare.   Is his name William ? "

" I don't know," said he ; " they call him Jim."

I tried to think of something I might say to that, but the simplicity of it defeated me.   W. Shakespeare, and they called him Jim !   Perhaps a fond mother had christened him William without any thought of plagiarism, but with the loving hope that one day—you never can tell—he might—— But I took it he had not, since now they called him Jim.   How merciless and unerring in its judgment the public is !

W. Shakespeare, and they called him Jim !

That is the subtlest form of criticism I have ever heard.

XXX

PRESTON BAGOT

How did they come into existence, these names of the country villages in England? Who had a hand in the making of them? Lowson Ford, Marston Meysey, Princes Risborough, Monks Risborough, Abbots Salford—in all parts, in all counties, you will find such names as bring pictures to your mind, full already of illumination, though never may you have seen the places themselves.

Even Preston Bagot has a sound about it, a sense of aloofness which stamps it once and forever with a joy of the country. But the names of cities—at least to me—mean nothing—Leeds, Birmingham, Manchester; only London has a sound of its own, a throb, a pulse, as of some great thing which is alive and moving. For the rest, there is not the faintest suggestion of choice between them. I would as soon go to Leeds as to Birmingham, as soon to Birmingham as to Manchester. Yet suggest but a visit to Mid-summer Norton, and though one may never have heard of the place in one's life, the very sound of it is an invitation.

I felt as sure I should like Preston Bagot as I was certain, when once I had come there, that it fulfilled all my expectations. The canal itself wound in and out, with countless turnings through meadows all in one generous garb of cowslips. Nature seemed never so lavish as this spring. If my compleat angler was a whole hospital to a medical student, then certainly the meadows near Preston Bagot and the woods in the Golden Valley were a whole book on botany to all those who might wish to read.

There are at least three, if not four or five, locks in the short distance between Lowson Ford and Preston Bagot. Their massive arms are the one feature without which the landscape of a canal would be much the same as any other. It is a fine moment, too, when the gates are shut and first the sluices are opened. It is not a matter of interest that I should count the times, but they were many, when I stood at the lock head and watched that first wild rush of water bubbling and bursting upwards like the eruption of a mighty volcano. There follows one moment then, when the surface of the water is prophetically still, as though before another and a greater outburst. But the second is never so mighty an upheaval as the first, and one by one they diminish until there is only that trembling shimmer as when

you see the quivering of heated air against strong
sunlight.

And slowly and slowly as she lifts in the rising
water beneath her, the thick rope fender on the nose
of the barge grinds with a gentle purr against the

worn lock gates.   These are the things you notice on
a barge.   The life is as quiet as that.

In some of the canals—as on this to Stratford—
so quiet is it that I wonder why they keep the lock-
houses in existence.   The work of the lock, indeed—
so much of it as there is—is left mostly to the lock-
keeper's wife, while he pursues a more remunerative

labour elsewhere. I doubt, in fact, whether these people are any longer in the pay of the canal company. Doubtless they rent the lock-house in the ordinary way of residence, and that is all.

Certainly at Preston Bagot the good woman, with an endeavour to supplement her husband's wages, had placed in that window which looked on to the canal a piece of paper on which was written, "Here Beer."

"There's something emphatic about that," said I, as the water raised us above the lock side and I found it staring at me.

"Look you, sur, that's a clever woman who put that there," said Eynsham Harry. "I never felt so close to a glass of beer in my life."

Whereupon he walked straight up to the lock-house door and knocked and the next minute had put himself in such proximity with it as allowed of no possible comparison. When he came back, he laid his hand upon his stomach and, with a wry smile on his face, said, "Here beer."

It was the only jest he attempted to make in all that journey. All other things he said, in which I found cause for laughter, were spoken in the characteristic seriousness of his nature, wherefore I was constrained to laugh at them within me, which is not wholly unenjoyable. A laugh with oneself is better than no laughter at all.

At some short distance from the lock-house the canal winds past the Manor Farm. It must be the finest example of half-timbered house there is left in England. Leicester's Hospital in Warwick seemed nothing to be compared with it.

"That's where I would live," said I, "if I had a dog's chance of it."

"You've said that, sur, of at least four houses since we be started."

"I shall go on saying it," said I, "as long as I see places like that. There's no harm in a man wishing to live where he can't. He hasn't to pay rent for it. If ever the misfortune befell me to find all the houses empty that I wished to live in, then I might be in a poor way."

"Well," said he, "'tis a thing I don't understand, living in houses. Why a man should put a roof over his head and make a wasp's nesty of it, wi' one room here and another room there, cutting

his space up into so many little pieces till there ain't
nothing left of it, that's a thing I never shall master.
It seems peculious to me."

Straightway, then, we began an argument which
lasted us all the way to Stratford.   And upon my
soul, I believe I got the worst of it.

XXXI

A CURE FOR TRIPPERS

IF I were to write of Stratford-on-Avon, I should be doing myself an irreparable injustice. I have one recollection of the place, but it is not associated with the time I went there on the *Flower of Gloster*. It will remain with me when I have long forgotten the architecture of the Memorial theatre and the Birthplace only clings faintly to my memory. I shall, in fact, always keep this recollection. It is of a lady dressed in white, seated in a pure-white gondola, propelled on the waters of the Avon by a gondolier all clothed in the same colour of virginal simplicity. Whenever I hear of Stratford, I think of that.

We should never have gone into the town this time, only that we needed supplies, for there was a long detour to be made before we came to Tewkesbury, upon which I had set my fancy. I wanted to make my way through Gloucestershire and the Cotswold Hills, and when it came to the next morning I shirked the brunt of that beating back ; for we must go over our own tracks almost to Birmingham

before we reached the junction of the Worcester
Canal.   Now I could not bear the thought of Birmingham again, so I sent Eynsham Harry back on the
barge with instructions to meet me next day at
Evesham.

"I'll join the canal there," said I, "and walk
along the tow-path towards Tewkesbury till we meet.
Have you ever traded on the Evesham Canal before?"

"No, sur, and 'tis my belief there's scarce a boat
goes along there now—not unless they be steam."

"Well, we can't make any mistake," said I
cheerfully.   "It's the river Avon, and I have it here
on a map ; 'tis navigable.   I shall walk straight on
from Evesham to Tewkesbury, and we shall meet
somewhere on the way."

We never met for some days, and then not until
I reached the wharf at Tewkesbury.   But little mis-
calculations like this will happen in the best of well-
planned journeys.   I should have missed almost the
best part of the adventure had I not buckled my
knapsack to my shoulder and set out from Stratford
that morning to walk to Evesham.

Now, if I had not done this—which in itself was
a treachery to all my scheme of a journey on a barge—
what should I not have lost ?   The fact of the matter
is, you must wear out at least one good pair of boots
if you are to know anything about the country in
which you live.   And once I had started, I could
have worn out ten pairs, only that it was arranged

that I should join the *Flower of Gloster* on the next day.

Seven miles out of Stratford you come to the little town of Bidford, with its bridge of many angles, which has borne the weight of Warwickshire traffic for four hundred and thirty years. In the days of King John, this same Bidford was the dowry of the Princess Joanne, when she was wed to Llewellyn, Prince of North Wales. Wonderful days were those, when a king could thrust his hand into the purse of his kingdom and draw forth such a dowry as this for his daughter's marriage. I wonder what would be the expression of feeling in Clapham if that idyllic spot were given away as dowry to a foreign prince ? You never know—it might become quite fashionable.

Yet, notwithstanding all the romance of its past history, Bidford has but little interest now. In the last twenty years it has been cruelly modernised, due, doubtless, to the fact that it has become the haunt of the Birmingham tripper. I am sure the tripper is a necessary evil. They must find the light of air after days of darkness in these black cities. But between the tripper and the ordinary traveller there is all that difference which exists between the wasp and the bee. The one goes about in swarms, eating and drinking on every possible occasion ; the other you will find but singly, heeding nothing but the pursuit of his labour.

I shall never forget the sight of a half-eaten

packet of dirty ham sandwiches lying cast away on one of the windows at Versailles. In every village, in every place of beauty or interest, there should be a poisoned public-house to catch the thirsty tripper. He would die as willingly as any wasp in a poisoned bottle; what is more, he would die in a complete sense of gratification, feeding himself until that moment when oblivion came softly to his side, and the packet of half-eaten sandwiches would drop from his lap on to the floor.

If only this were done, there would be no orange peel in Petit Trianon, and Bidford might still have been a dowry fit for any princess.

XXXII

AN OLD NUNNERY

Soon after I had left Bidford I met two old women with white sun-bonnets and sun-browned faces, who directed me on my way to Evesham.

"Turn first turn to the right," said they in a chorus, "and keep on away past the nunnery."

"The nunnery?" said I.

"The nunnery," said they, and on I went with quickening steps.

At first sight of it, this old nunnery in Abbots Salford almost took my breath away. It was an annihilation of all time. I was back again—if indeed I had ever existed in that period—in the days of Queen Elizabeth. Had a man walked down the grey slabbed path to the lichgate entrance in a silk hat and a tail coat, I should straightway have clapped him into armour or blotted him out of my sight altogether.

It would seem that scarcely a stone has been altered and, except for a small addition which was made to the house some two or three hundred years ago, now well hidden by trees, it must be just the same as it was in the days even long before Elizabeth, when the little nuns kept their farm and fed their poor and saved their money.

The floor within the great high hall is stone— huge slabs of grey toned rich with yellow age, which make you shudder to think of the coldness of the winter nights. I rambled all over it from cellar to roof, paying my sixpence—which is the charge—to the little girl who, thank God, so unlike a guide, took me from room to room with a whispered "Would you like to see the priest's hole?" "Would you like to see the dormitories?"

I liked to see everything, and I think the dormitories, where all those little sisters slept like sparrows close beneath the roof, was the most redolent of the history of the place. It was one colossal chamber, stretching with its massive beams from one gable to another. Here, in one long row, there was accommodation for at least thirty sleepers ; for, as I strongly suspect, they had no beds raised from the ground, but slept on straw mattresses ranged along the floor.

At each end of this great room, lighted, not with small dormer windows, but fine, high mullioned spaces that looked wide across the breadth of country and flooded the interior with light, there was a recess where doubtless the sisters slept in charge of all the little nuns.

I cannot help calling them little, for however big she may be in stature, a nun is slight in mind —a child, whose thoughts will never grow into womanhood, who will never know a greater pang than death, which indeed she woos as though he were a lover.

Two hours I spent within the nunnery, peopling each room, for it was a place that gave you a thousand stories without one effort of yours in the creation of them.

Only the chapel disappointed me, for that is still used as the Roman Catholic place of worship in the district, having all the signs of modern Catholicism about it—the cheap finery, the gaudy altar cloth, the ill-painted pictures of the journey of the cross around the walls.

When once I had seen that, then the spell of the place seemed to be broken and I left it, wishing

I might have carried my memory of it away without just that one discordant note.

Yet I suppose it is better to believe than to feel.

The few who come there to that little chapel gain a thousand times more comfort from their Mass and Benediction than should I have done in keeping the feeling of the place alive in my memory by its absence.

" The selfishness in this world," said I, as I walked back to the lichgate entrance, " the selfishness in this world is abominable."

Now, I have always noticed that when a man's conscience makes it imperative that he should accuse himself, he does so in the meanest way possible. He generalises. " The selfishness in this world," says he. Had he to credit himself with a virtue, he would give the world none of it, and phrase his sentence in a very different way.

XXXIII

FLADBURY MILL

AT Evesham begins the so-called navigable part of
the Avon. I knew directly I had reached it that I
had all the walk to Tewkesbury before me, for
Eynsham Harry was quite right—nothing but steam
barges could make their way in that water. The
tow-path had long been overgrown ; only here and
there could I discover signs of it.

So I put my best foot foremost and reached
Fladbury that evening, where I agreed with myself
to stay the night.

There was something about Fladbury Mill and
Fladbury Ferry which brought me back to those
days when I was a child. Had I spent the first ten
years of my life at Fladbury Mill, I should have had
a more splendid time even than I had in a house on
the edge of a wood, which fulfilled for me then all
the great mysterious qualities of a real forest. For
in Fladbury Mill and the river running by it, in the
broad, tumbling weir, in the secret waters, and the
deep, deep lock behind the mill, I could see all the

FLADBURY
MILL

possibilities of a thousand inventions, adventures that would have lasted well through the long summer holidays, and held all their interest and enchantment until the term be sped again.

Instead of Mrs Wicks, who surreptitiously used to give me of her gloriously home-made toffee from the buttered frying-pan in which she was wont to make it, I can see Mrs Izod, the ferry-woman at Fladbury, supplying me with radishes from her baskets. This does not please me in contemplation quite so well as the place itself, for radishes would never take the place of home-made toffee—never! But all the rest of it, that was full of tales just waiting to be spun out of the palpitating imagination of some child living at the mill. Maybe they are being told now; maybe they were being told that day when I was there, by the two children, a boy and girl, who were rowing up the river in a leaky old boat—quite possibly those tales were being told then; those adventures were afoot under my very eyes, only I had grown too old to realise them. I am glad, however, that I was not so old as that I could not see their possibilities of them myself.

With just a boat, such as those two children had, how real could Red Indians become in their birch-bark canoes at Fladbury Ferry! What pirates' ships could not be made out of any old thing that floated on the waters of a river in such a place as that!

For some long time—an hour, it may well have

been—I sat down by the ferry-slip and thought of all the splendid things that could be done with only two essential possessions—just childhood and a boat. How easily might that sleepy mill become the frowning Tower of London, to which, by water and the Traitor's Gate, all prisoners were brought for execution! How easily might all the stirring history of England be written through again at Fladbury Mill, with just childhood and a boat!

For childhood, like Nature, can make history with whatsoever comes to hand. It is only when he has reached to man's estate that a child must build castles, set precious stones in crowns, and pave the streets with gold before he can write a year into the book of history.

And Fladbury Mill is such a spot where a pair of children, unbridled and free, could set all history a-humming with their deeds. I wish I had been born at Fladbury Mill! How many thousands of times Mrs Izod, as, lazily, she pulled the ferry-boat from one bank to another, would not have found herself attacked by a pirate's cutter, boarded, and every passenger thereon made to deliver up their wealth and walk the plank! It would only be pretence, that walking the plank, I have no doubt, but still, a matter easily accomplished while one looked the other way, lest in their pretence the illusion had been spoiled.

This is but a little of all that Fladbury brought

to me as I sat by the ferry-slip and watched the
water tumbling down the weir.   I even caught myself speculating on a race between two flat flecks of
foam as, collecting at the bottom of the weir, they
started off down the river, neck and neck.

Here, too, the swallows were skimming the
water ; up and down, up and down, with endless
passages, never seeking rest.   I could hear Bellwattle
in my imagination asking, with wide eyes of wonder,
" Do they *never* sit down ? "   But it seems as if they
never do.

And then—the more mature, perhaps thereby
the less complete of all the pleasures I found in
Fladbury—I sat on a bank of the river where a crab
tree glowed with pink in fullest bloom, and listened
to a trio of three nightingales, who sang and sang and
sang until it seemed that not a note was left in all the
compass of music which they had not touched.

I have often wondered whether the nightingale
was really so fine a songster as repute would have
him.   Sometimes it has seemed that only because
he sang when all the rest of the world was silent
has his voice won him a spurious reputation.   And
when I have heard the notes of a blackbird rising
above all the other sounds of day, I have seriously
been in two ways about it.   But that evening at
Fladbury, when the sun was dropping fast behind
the square tower of Fladbury church in the distance,
I was left in no doubt of it.   A thrush was singing

somewhere. I heard the blackbird's note as well;
but they none of them could match my trio. There
were passages in that song which the mere transcribing
to the written stave would desecrate for ever. For
they sing that music which you would rather never
hear again unless by such executants.

It was while I sat there listening that an old
woman—sun-bonneted as most of them are—came
round the river meadows gathering sticks and dandelions. In her passing from one field to another,
she had to climb a stile, but refused all help of mine
in surmounting it. First she handed over her sticks,
then her apron-full of dandelions, lastly she climbed
herself.

"You're very independent," said I.

" 'Tis a good thing to be, sur, while 'ee can.
If you be round these parts next year, maybe I'll be
glad to taking help of 'ee."

"And what are you doing?" I asked. "What
are the dandelions for?"

"They be for wine, sur. My old man likes his
draught of it after the hot days. He says it be as
good as any cider, the way I makes it."

"And how do you make it?"

"Three quarts of blossoms," said she, " to a gallon
of water, three pounds of sugar, the juice of lemonses
and oranges, and when loo-warm mix yeast."

"When's it ready for drinking?"

"In three months, sur—three months to brew.

There be some as drinks it in a week or so, but I keep mine three months, and I have had some as has been in brew a year. 'Twas well called wine, my old man said—he got quite jolly over it one day, he did."

" And did you scold him for that ? " said I.

" Well, I did begin, sur ; but he did say such good things about the wine as I'd made, I couldn't find it in me heart. And he made us all laugh, he did, the way he said things. I've never seen him the same like it since."

" P'raps you don't make the wine so well," said I.

" Oh, sur, indeed I does my best."

" Then I expect you wouldn't really be so very sorry if you saw him like that again."

" Well," said she, and her head hung very thoughtfully, " I sometimes wonders perhaps if he did once take a little drop of it too much, I might know 'twas to his liking."

" It's a difficult matter," said I, and I hung my head as well, " but it's always the way in this world" ; and here I spoke very sententiously, as though I would add philosophy to ease her difficulties. " It's hard to know," said I ; " you want to make it to his liking, and he never tells you what he thinks of it unless he takes a drop too much. Well, we all have problems like this to settle. Life's not so easy as it looks."

" Indeed, it is not, sur," said she, and, bobbing

FLADBURY FERRY

me a curtsey, she picked up her sticks and her apron-full of dandelions. I stood and watched her till she hobbled out of sight.

" My God ! " said I to myself, " if the best of us could be no more beset than that ! " and I pictured the prayer she would pray that night to help her in her difficulty. Surely the essence of all comedy and tragedy must be in prayer. If only one could hear them all !

By this time my trio had ended their choiring and had left the crab tree. I walked back in an evening silence then through the meadows, and Mrs Izod ferried across from the village slip to the mill to fetch me.

XXXIV

WOOL-GATHERING

SOME years ago, Nafford Mill was burnt to the
ground. No, not to the ground, for the four pink-
washed walls of it still stand with their sightless
windows facing the evening sun like a palace built
upon a Venetian canal. All the interior is gutted.
The charred beams have been left to rot upon the
ground ; the great iron wheels and shafts, distorted
into wild shapes by the fierce flames that embraced
them, are lying there now in a debris of bricks and
mortar. Its only roof is the open vault of heaven.
Now the heavy mill-wheel is quite still, the water
trickles over its slimy plates, for the chains are
all rusted and broken and it will never revolve
again.

Yet notwithstanding all this devastation, the wide
stretch of the Avon here would be incomplete without its mill at Nafford. It stands there at the foot
of a steep green slope of grass where on the crest a
small thatched farm-house lies down in the shadows
of the apple orchard and gazes through its dim

latticed windows to the purple heights of Bredon Hill.

I suppose in its days of labour, Nafford Mill lent more to its surroundings than it does now ; then I have no doubt the splashing of the water as it turned the old mill-wheel, the gentle whir of the machinery within, and all those peaceful sounds which accom-

panied the daily grinding of its heavy stones, made such music in the place as, to those who know their Avon well, must now seem desolate in all its silence. But to one who has never seen it otherwise, Nafford Mill could not well be more splendid than it is. I liked its lonely air, its sightless windows, and its silent wheel. The walls, as they stand deep down in the clearest water, might well be made of marble when the sun is shining on them. And all that fulness of apple-blossom which spreads in the orchard around the hill only adds to the almost transparent suggestion that it gives. Indeed, through the higher windows as you look upwards from below, the blue sky glistens, and it seems not like a building of solid brick at all,

ECKINGTON BRIDGE

but an enchanted palace full of the light of air and gleaming sunshine.

From Fladbury I came to Nafford, by way of Eckington Bridge and Eckington village, and much as I enjoyed the company of Eynsham Harry, yet they were glorious were those few days when I walked alone down the banks of the Avon.

Of the countless bridges I passed in that journey, I think Eckington is the most wonderful, the most picturesque of all. It must date back some considerable number of years before that of Bidford, for even now it is the only means of transport between Pershore and Tewkesbury with the exception of one single ferry across the river. For awhile I stood in one of its niches where the cautious pedestrian may secure himself against the close passing of the heavy traffic, and there I watched the waters below me flowing onwards and onwards to the ultimate sea.

There is no place in the world so suitable to reflection as the bridge which spans a gently flowing stream. For whether it be wool-gathering, as I strongly suspect was much the case with me, or whether it be a flight into the highest realms of philosophy, it is equally pleasant, equally the place above all others. Herr Teufelsdröckh, had he stood upon a bridge over the Rhine looking down into the flowing waters beneath him instead of being seated in his garret beneath the stars, would have arrived at a more far-reaching philosophy even than that of clothes. There is something in flowing water so constantly and compellingly changing, something which both arrests yet carries on the feeblest of imaginations, that to stand upon a bridge and watch its even, passing ripples must impel the mind to think, and to think, moreover, of things made mysteries by the mutable laws of life. It is coming from whither? It is going whence? And therewith your mind begins its journey from the far-off mountains to the distant sea, until, lost in the limitlessness of a dim horizon, you inevitably return unto yourself, the minute yet living atom standing upon that bridge in the silent country—you, the smallest speck in this great ocean of space, who, in the flash of an eye, can cast your mind into the distant corners of the earth and yet are there, still standing as I was upon the bridge at Eckington.

It meant nothing—I got no further ; yet at moments I had that feeling which Eynsham Harry had so deftly described—I felt that I was on the verge of one of the greatest secrets of the world. It seemed to grow so simple until, from the sheer greatness of its simplicity, it escaped my grasp, and once more I found myself wildly struggling in a seething whirlpool of complexities.

It was no good. I knew that I could arrive at nothing, for I was no more than as one particle in all that volume of water which had passed beneath me as I stood upon the bridge of Eckington ; I was no more than a drop being carried on and on, just capable of locating myself, of speculating upon my existence while in the narrow river of life, then lost again, perhaps lost forever in the limitless eternity of the sea.

I left the bridge at last. My wool-gathering, or, as no doubt I may have called it, my philosophy, had brought me nowhere. However much it strives, the mind cannot escape the body ; however far it travels into space, it must return. In no little feeling of the despair of it all, I walked on then into the village.

At the very entrance of it there stands a Roman cross, around which, on summer evenings, the old people sit and gossip. Sometimes they call them butter-crosses, for here, some two hundred years ago, they came on butter-market days to sell their wares.

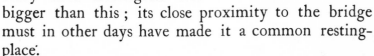

With the exception of its old Norman church, Ecking-ton is just the quiet Wor-cestershire village, having no particular beauties to recom-mend it. But in its day, I fancy that Eckington was bigger than this ; its close proximity to the bridge must in other days have made it a common resting-place.

Through Eckington, then, I passed on to Nafford, where in the little thatched farm cottage I was given a dish of tea, and set out afterwards to climb to the summit of Bredon Hill.

Half-way up this hill, from the crest of which it would almost seem that the whole of England lay stretched before your eyes, stands Woolas Hall with its fine old tapestries and its minstrel's gallery. I gather this information from the book of a Mr Charles Showell, who, more fortunate than I, was admitted to see the place, and has drawn in his book of the Avon a picture of the fine old gables of which I could catch but a glimpse while the groom was informing me that only friends of the house were allowed to come within.

This, as I believe I have said before, is quite as it should be. If an Englishman's home really be his castle and his flag is not concealed within the boot-cupboard but flying royally and egotistically from his flag-staff, then the intrusion of a stranger within his gates must be little less than an abomination. I certainly deserved to be turned away. In these matters a vagabond deserves everything he gets. So really I never saw Woolas Hall; but what with a glimpse over the coachman's shoulder and such imagination as not even an English gentleman can deprive me of, I can picture the glorious place that it is.

Yet better than any mansion was the sight of the country from the summit of Bredon Hill.

"God," said I, as I stood up there and gazed across the wide stretches of fields so many hundred feet below me, "God is more generous of his pleasures than is any man." Which, by the way, is what one only has the right to expect.

XXXV

APPLE BLOSSOM

It was a whole village wrapped in apple bloom. And in the light of that sunset, like snow on the mountains, it was burnished with a glow of pink. You could scarcely see the cottages for all those sheets of blossoms ; indeed, at a distance, as I walked towards it, only the square tower of the old Norman church rose above this mass of burning white.

This is the village of Little Cumberton in the month of May. It is a colony of apple orchards. They surround every cottage, make the greater acreage of every farm, and almost every garden, it seemed, had one or two trees to bear them fruit.

To add to this, the cottages themselves, half-timbered, are washed white between the beams ; the trunks of the apple trees are all painted with lime as well. Never did I see even linen more spotlessly white than was this little village. in the shadow of Bredon Hill. If ever Nature can be said, where the presence of man is unavoidable, to look immaculate, it was here. But immaculate is not really a good word.

It has so often been used to describe the modern dandy in all his glory of attire, that it has lost the meaning for which alone I use it.   Little Cumberton was

immaculate, but only to those who know what I really would infer.

I stayed the night there in an old farm-house in the heart of the village.   Their garden also had its apple trees ; it had its tulips, its forget-me-nots and its Aubrietia beside. The farmer's wife had her eye for colour. But she had planted her tulips in lines so straight that when your eye ran along them as they stood beneath the windows, you could see how uneven were the old walls of the house itself.

The latticed window of my bedroom looked over clouds of apple blossom to the narrow street of the village. I asked that my bed might be moved across the room and placed directly under the window. This was done with all the willingness in the world ; and when it came to ten o'clock, I retired, undressed, and lay beneath the clothes beside the open window watching the light of the moon as she drifted through a fleet of clouds which seemed to lie at anchor over Bredon Hill.

There is as much a joy in sleeping close to Nature as there is in being close to her awake. Again and again I closed my eyes, when there would creep into my mind the never-ceasing stir of traffic which echoes through every hour of a London night. And though it was now more than three weeks since I had heard it, the sound of it plainly reached my ears. It was not until I had opened my eyes again to watch the silent traffic of the moon across those dark streets of the sky, that the real stillness of the world came back to me.

The last thing I remember was the soft cry of an owl, and then, perhaps I only imagined it, I thought

I saw something heavy and white fly cumbersomely out of the darkness of the trees across the light of the moon and into the darkness once more. I may only have imagined it, for the next moment I was asleep.

In the morning I woke early. The sun was on

my face, a slight breeze was tapping the branch of a climbing rose against the window pane.

I turned on my side and looked out. The village was still asleep. Presently I heard a dog barking—those short, excited yaps as when he is eager about his business. Then there came a flock of sheep, followed by an old shepherd and the dog himself. The shepherd was taking them up to their pasture on the hills. A little cloud of dust from the white road wrapped around them as they walked. Before

they reached the end of the street it folded them
out of sight. I heard the dog barking now and
again in the distance, and before the sound of it had
died away, there came the sharp snap of a window-
catch let loose. I heard the rattle of the latticed
panes as they swung back against the wall of the
house. It was the village stirring—just awake.

XXXVI

TEWKESBURY

TEWKESBURY has not suffered as have Banbury or Bidford. It is as old as the hills, you might say—and without fear of hopelessly being plagiarist, for the hills surround it. So far as I understand, rather than

having increased its trade, Tewkesbury has lost it. Some of the old mills are empty now—the wharves are deserted.

There I met Eynsham Harry again, faithfully in

charge of the *Flower of Gloster*, waiting with an even
and contented mind for me to fulfil my promise and
turn up eventually by the canal side. When he saw
me approaching, he came forward to meet me with
that strange lateral swing of the hands which all
bargees have acquired from long walking between
the locks. It seems to help them to their pace, for
they swing to every step with an automatic action
which is inseparable from their stride.

"I told 'ee, sur," said he first thing, "that
'twas only steam-boats they'd take down from
Evesham."

"It makes no matter," said I. "It isn't because I
like boating so much that I'd have anything to say
against Shanks's mare. She's an amiable beast, and 'll
go mostly anywhere."

"You rode, then, sur? And here have I been
wasting my sympathies on you, thinking how you'd
be a-walking. But who might be Mr Shanks? I've
never heard of 'en."

I explained. I should have thought the phrase
might have reached him ; but they have queer phras-
ing of their own. Not that I heard much of it from
Eynsham Harry. I often thought that notwithstanding he could neither read nor write, yet he was
rather a cut above the rest—perhaps because they
could.

"Well," said I, "there are three more days before
our month is up. I'm going to take a stroll round

the town, and then we'll start.   I want to go through
the Golden Valley and then on to Lechlade."

" I'll get provisions, sur, and whenever you're
ready, that am I."

So I walked round the old town of Tewkesbury.
It is full of strange crevices, and at every turn there
looms above the house-tops the splendid tower of its
historic abbey.   A lot of the work in it, dating from
the twelfth century, still remains in wonderful pre-
servation.   But thank heavens, I know nothing about
these things, and cannot even talk of architraves and
bastions in such a way as would make this chronicle
too dull for any but an architect's apprentice.

The sight of it delighted me, none the less.   At
every corner as it rose above the old Tudor buildings,
it reminded me of Rouen.   How well, indeed, they
have preserved their atmosphere there.   It is the
town as it was, and Tewkesbury is much the same.

There are passages in the streets there, thrust
secretly in between the houses where you would least
expect them.   Glance down them, and you might
almost believe the sixteenth century were back again.
Old half-timbered gables lean across the narrow spaces
until they well-nigh touch each other.   All this is
bound to create a sense of mystery even to the dullest
imagination.

I wished then, when once I had seen a little of it,
that I had time to see it all.   It is so closely written
into the pages of England's history that it is a lesson,

if it be nothing else.   And I for one, at least, have
need of such teaching.   But having walked down
two or three streets and being come but half way

down a fourth, I saw a crowd of men and women
gathered round some man, to whom they listened
while he talked with flowery gestures and that so-
called persuasive tone of voice.   Now, had the kings

of England all been buried at Tewkesbury, I would rather have stopped to listen in this crowd than see a whole row of their tombs.

The man who can hold a crowd is worth listening to, whatever rubbish he may be talking, and it is mostly rubbish that you hear. I stayed once to listen to an orator in Hyde Park.

" Mr Heggarty will now speak to you on Home Rule," said a voice, and thus the new-comer was introduced to his audience. For half an hour he held them spell-bound. They turned open mouths to him, swallowing every word. Yet for half an hour that man never finished one sentence, never made one complete statement in all the words that came between his lips.

" He's a grand speaker," a man in the crowd whispered to me in an awed voice.

" He is indeed," said I : " what's he saying ? "

" I don't know," he replied abstractedly—" he's talking about Home Rule " ; and then his mouth opened once more as he returned the fulness of his attention.

"I wonder," said I, as I walked away, " I wonder if that's the secret of success in the noble calling of politics ? "

But this was no politician in the High Street of Tewkesbury. He was none the less striving to convince his public of what God knows he could never have believed himself. He was offering painlessly to extract their corns with the filthiest instrument I have ever seen in my life.

"Ladies and gentlemen," he was saying as I came up ; and that was wise of him, they liked that very much.   One and all, they felt constrained to listen when he addressed them so.

"Ladies and gentlemen," and with his flowery gestures waving his awful forceps about him he kept back all small children, who crawled in through people's legs, "if any one of you is sufferin' the tortures as come from sweaty feet, let him sit down here openly on this chair as I've got for the purpose, let him sit down and have his collosities painlessly removed.   I don't mind whether they're hard or soft, white or black, let him sit down here, and in less than thirty seconds he shall have his collosity in his hand, roots, fibres, and all."

Then, as he surveyed the crowd for a likely patient, his comprehensive glance fixed steadily on me.   I felt a sudden consciousness of my feet at once.   They say, if you look at a person's boots it unnerves them.   It is sufficient for a chiropodist to look you in the face.   What is more, I am sure that everyone else in that crowd upon whom his wandering eye chanced to fall, felt just the same as I.   In fact, I saw them gaze down nervously at their boots, and if the glance continued, they would then stare at the buildings opposite, as though they were more concerned with what was happening there. I stared at the buildings opposite myself.

He was a greasy fellow, this journeyman. With his soft black hat, his long yellow hair, and his black frock-coat, he was much more like a photographer than the chiropodist he called himself.

"George Schofield is my name," I heard him saying presently, when I felt it safe to return the full mead of my attention. "I'm a professor of chiropody—a surgeon chiropodist. Now, when I say professor," he continued, "I don't mean a self-titled idiot. You've 'ad some people coming 'ere to Tewkesbury—I know 'em—I've met 'em. I've stood in the crowd same as you're doing now, and I've 'eard the nonsense they talk. Professors!" His contempt was large, comprehensive. A young farm-hand, meeting his glance, withered visibly beneath it. "Why, I've seen one of them almost bleed a poor woman to death, the way he hacked at her. Now, that's not my way. With this little instrument in my 'and," he held out the rusty forceps, that all might see it who chose, "I'm an artist. I've had my degree at a college. I'm not only known in Stroud and Gloucester—I'm known all over the country. I've extracted collosities from nearly all the crowned heads of Europe."

I suppose wearing a crown upon your head has much the same effect as wearing boots upon your feet. It was the first time I had ever heard it, and, in any case, is not a nice thing to think about.

"Well, now," he went on, " if anyone has a collosity and wants to be operated on, let him not be ashamed. If he's done no sin let him not be ashamed. Lady or gentleman, there ain't no harm in any of these people seeing your feet. Don't be modest about it. Why, I've got a letter 'ere—there's 'ardly a post but what I don't get one—from a lady I operated on in London." He began feeling first in one pocket, then in another. " It was from a lady in 'Ornsey. I took three corns out of 'er one foot. Now, where is that letter ? Well, any'ow, she thanked me for what I'd done—thanked me from the bottom of 'er 'eart. That was the way she put it—'from the bottom of my 'eart.' 'Walking,' she said, ' is a pleasure. Where before I used to drive in my motor,' she said, ' now I can walk.'"

" Dommed if I'd walk an' I'd a motor," said some envious fellow in the crowd.

" You wouldn't," said Schofield ; " but these ladies in London likes a little walk now and then—keeps 'em fit. They don't get no other exercise. Paying an afternoon visit, they like a walk sometimes.'

Especially, thought I, those ladies in Hornsey.

" Well—'oo's going to take a seat ? " persisted the professor. " You don't mean to tell me that with all the work you 'ave to do, gentlemen, keeping the 'ome going, that you don't 'ave corns ! Why, there

was a gentleman in Stroud—retired, 'e was—retired—
living on 'is own. 'E never 'ad no work to do at all,
and 'e 'ad six corns—three on one foot, three on the
other. 'You sit down, Mr Capel,' I said—that
was 'is name—'you sit down, and I'll take 'em out
for you in as many seconds.' He didn't believe me
at first. 'I've been suffering with these,' said he,
'for four years,' he said. 'You'll only suffer six
more seconds,' said I. So 'e sat down, and in a whiff
they was all lying on the floor by the side of 'em.
'Ah,' said he, 'you've done very well with those
corns, Schofield; but I've got something even you
can't tackle.' 'What's that?' said I. 'An ingrowing
toe-nail,' said he. 'Sit down there again,' said I, 'and
I'll have it out in two minutes.' 'What!' said he.
'Yes,' said I.

"Well, I took it out, and he was proud of it; he
was going to put that along with the six corns in his
pocket to show to his wife when he got 'ome. But
I stopped 'im there. 'Oh no,' said I, 'if you take
the toe-nail, I must 'ave the collosities.' So I got
'em—we split the difference, and 'ere they are'';
and, taking a bottle from a black bag on the ground,
he held up those touching remembrances of his art,
which, when he shook the bottle, floated nebulously
in some dirty liquid before our eyes.

There comes a moment when even an orator of his
persuasion loses hold upon his audience. It was at
this moment that Mr Schofield, surgeon chiropodist,

lost his hold upon me.   I edged my way out of the
crowd, and, far down the street I could hear his voice

still raised in tireless eloquence.   At last there was a
lull. I looked back over my shoulder.   His soft black
hat no longer rose above the crowd surrounding him.

I guessed, then, he was operating at last. The artist was at work. I hurried on with a sharp pain suddenly tingling in my feet.

Now, of course, I wish that I had seen more of Tewkesbury instead of listening to the cajoleries of this journeyman chiropodist. Yet in those two short hours before we started upon the last stage of our journey, I saw much to make that time a memory. There is great nobility in it. The ring of battle still lingers in its name. They say Queen Margaret weeps o' nights in Bloody Meadow for her son. If the departed spirits still cherish the sorrows which they knew on earth, then I am sure she must, for Tewkesbury is full of the spirits of the past.

XXXVII

THE GOLDEN VALLEY

WHEN you join the Thames and Severn Canal at
Stroud, it is but twenty-eight miles and a few odd
furlongs before you come to Inglesham, where the
water of the canal joins the Isis and all signs of the
tow-path are lost to you for ever.   But those twenty-
eight miles are worth a thousand for the wealth of
their colour alone.

Immediately you have come to Brimscombe Basin
and the high land, studded with the grey Gloucestershire houses, begins to rise at either side the canal, it
is no longer the English scenery you might expect,
but like mountain villages in Switzerland, thousands
of feet above the level of the sea.   I have seen villages
in the heart of the Apennines which reminded me of
Chalford and St Mary's crossing.   The mills and the
factories with blue slate roofs make a colour against that
golden distance, the distance of the Golden Valley, to
which, through all those little villages on the hill-sides,
you feel you are always leading, slowly and surely, like
a miner who knows that the day will come when he

shall strike his reef.   There is an aura of gold everywhere.   The distance is no longer blue—that is more
the colour of all the nearer foreground.   But away
beyond it there is a mist of gold into which all tones
and shadows melt like metal cast into a furnace.
Mills and factories, blue slate roofs and grey houses!
All this sounds impossible; but it is true!

Wherever there is a field in which pasture is left to
grow, there the grass is of a golden green, accentuated,
there is no doubt, by the sheets of cowslips which are
spread everywhere in every open space.

Yet this is but the beginning of the Golden Valley,
the long courtyard to that garden through which you
must pass before you come to the great gates which
give you entrance to this deep valley of gold.   And
all along by the side of this paved courtyard there
grow in broad white feathered masses the flowers of
cow-parsnip.   At one spot, on a pathway the other
side of the canal, there is a door set in a wall that the
path itself may continue.   Here was the greatest
cluster of all.   I pointed them out to Eynsham Harry.

" Nature has a wonderful eye for effect," said I,
" when she sows her flowers.   Look through that
doorway.   Where could you get a better place for a
mass of those cow-parsnips?"

His eye followed my hand.

" 'Tis the fault of most people, sur," he replied,
" when they plants gardens, to have things in rows, so
you can count how many there be.   I never had a

garden myself—we none of us do, a-boating,—but when I sets some cowslips or blue-bells in a bowl on the cabin, I puts them all in a lump.   They looks better that way."

I remembered then how many a cabin roof I had seen decked with a bowl of wild-flowers.   I had seen birds in cages too, carried through their own fields and meadows, chafing against their captivity.   I asked him if he could explain that.

He shook his head.

" Look you, sur," he said presently.   " There be some persons in this world as have no more sense of the feeling of dumb things than what they'd have of a stone.   What's more, they'd think you was daftie if you said them birds weren't made to sing in cages, and had no more taste for it than you and I would have for a week's job on the treadmill."

" 'Tis more customary," said I, " for them to call you a sentimentalist—though no doubt your people mean much the same when they call you daft.   Both accusations are supposed to make you feel ashamed of yourself."

" Well, sur, if I could open the doors of half the cages I sees on the boats, I wouldn't mind how ashamed I felt.   Most like I should get over it, which is more'n the bird 'ud do if he was left in the cage.'

Soon after Chalford, the grey houses with their blue slate roofs grow fewer in number, the hills at each side become higher ; there are broader pasture

fields ; a stray farm or a lock-house is all you can see
of human habitation.   In the nearer distance, the
dense woods spread over the rolling land and, like
an army in glittering mail, with golden trappings

and with coloured plumes, they march down the hill-
sides to the water's edge.

This part of the country must be the most
luxuriant in the whole of England.   In a half-hour's
ramble through those woods while Eynsham Harry
was preparing the mid-day meal, I counted seventeen
various sorts of wild-flowers then in bloom.   There

were bluebells and orchis—those deep-red purple
orchis with their spotted leaves which, in the midst
of the dark violet of the bluebells, made such colours
as they wore in the great days of Rome's Empire.
Could the imperial toga have been indeed as imperial
as these?

I found the cuckoo-pint as well, its livid finger
in that pale fragile sheath of green. There were
nettles, red and white, but with such bloom as would
shame many a hot-house plant in London. Veronica
was there, with its tiny blossoms that might match
the cobalt of any Chinese dynasty you liked to
name. Garlick I found, and primroses hiding from the
heat of May, the last I knew that I should see that
year. The violets grew so thickly, I could scarce
but tread them down. Ground ivy crawled in every
open space and, with roots dipping in the cool water,
there were forget-me-nots, king-cups with blossoms
of metallic gold and lesser celandine, apeing the
glories of their sovereign.

I found strawberries in blossom and the purple
flowers of common bugle. There was Herb-Robert
with its brilliant scented leaf, stitchwort and salvia.
I have no doubt I missed a great many more.
There must have been knotted figwort, there must
have been white and purple comfrey. I saw no
plants of willow herb, yet they must have been there
as well. But I had no time to count them all, their
abundance was so overwhelming.

And with all these jewelled flowers, imagine a valley of gold. The leaves of the countless trees all set before you in the golden flush of youth; the fields upon the other bank dipped in the gold of a myriad buttercups and cowslips ; the sunlight streaming on it all from a cloudless sky in May—gold—all gold—a priceless valley paved in gold and precious stones.

When I came out from the shadows of those woods into the sunshine again, I could only stand and wonder, wonder what any man would say—his first words—if on a magic carpet I could whip him up from the grey streets and plant him there where I stood. It would probably be something in the nature of blasphemy, but acceptable nevertheless to the God who made it all—far more acceptable as a genuine meed of praise than any prayer of thanksgiving grudgingly offered in a consecrated church.

I returned silently to the barge ; as silently sat down to my mid-day meal. Presently I became conscious of the fact that Eynsham Harry was watching me while I eat.

" What is it ? " I asked.

" I be waiting for you to taste that dish, sur," said he.

It was a dish of green vegetable, looking as much like spinach as anything else. I thought it was spinach.

" Where did you get it ? " I inquired.

" Would you be so good as to just taste it, sur," he repeated.

I obeyed, looking up at him as I did so with that pensive expression which I am sure all professional tasters must adopt. You must put on an expression when you specialise. It is part of your uniform, whether it be in the tea factory, the pulpit, or the house of parliament. All specialists are actors.

"Tastes like asparagus," said I. "Where did you get it from?"

Still he would not tell me.

"You like it, sur?" he persisted.

I tried another mouthful.

"It's better than asparagus," said I.

"Put a little pepper wi' it, sur."

I put a little pepper and tasted again.

"By Jove," said I, "it's damned good! Where *did* you get it?"

He pointed to a line of hedge half-way up the hill.

"There be hops growing up on that hedge, sur," said he; "these that you're eating be the young shoots, cut off about six inches from the top and boiled the same as other greens. In the month of May we takes 'en whenever we can. The wilder the better."

"I'll remember that," said I; and I have, but can find no hedges in London where the wild hop-vine grows. I shall think of it, however, when next May-time comes. I shall surely taste that dish again.

XXXVIII

THE GOLDEN VALLEY—*continued*

For more than three miles the canal divides the
wooded hills, a band of silver drawn through this

valley of gold. Lock by lock it mounts the gentle
incline until it reaches the pound to Sapperton tunnel,
and at the summit spreads into a wide basin before it

passes into the last lock, some few hundred yards
before the tunnel's mouth.

The whole way from Stroud upwards is almost
deserted now.   We only met one barge in the whole

journey. An old lady with capacious barge bonnet was standing humming quietly to herself at the tiller. That was the only boat we found on those waters. The locks are, however, good ; some of them have only just been made within the last few years. But

the draught of water is bad ; in some places we just floated, and no more. It was stern work for Fanny then. There were times when I thought the tow-line must give way, the strain upon it was so great.

In one short pound more shallow than the rest, we came upon two little boys bathing. One was swimming manfully, making great pace and great commotion, struggling as though for dear life; while

the other, knee-deep in the shallow water, stood by
in undisguised admiration. I strongly suspect the
swimmer had one leg upon the bottom. I could
always swim so well like that myself. I know too
how splendid it looks, for if you make a splash
enough there is not a soul can see.

After our meal we went on through the rest of
this wonderful valley. It was golden to the last.
Even in the water itself the weeds grew more luxuri-
antly than I have seen in any river. In and out of the
forests of trailing weed the fish moved mysteriously,
like mermaids in a fairy-tale. It was all a fairy-tale
beneath that water. There were dense growths, and
then clear spaces on to which the sunshine fell in
brilliant patches. The pen of Hans Andersen could

have found many a story in that magic country beneath the still water of the canal.

At the top of the valley, looking down between the hills through a lattice-work of apple blossom, stands the Bricklayers Arms, a little inn with two or three houses clustered round it. An old man there described to me the opening of the tunnel in the reign of George IV. He had not seen it himself.

" My big grandfather "—this was how he told it to me—" my big grandfather, the day the tunnel was opened, he was walking down the tow-path, and he met a feller coming along, and he said to my big grandfather, ' Where are you going, my man ? ' ' I'm going to see the king,' he says. ' I am the king,' says the man, and gives him a guinea ; and when he looked at the head on the coin, I'm dommed if it worn't."

It was rather nice, that little touch of human incredulity. I can see him comparing the likeness with that of the head on the coin, catching the face in profile before he finally made up his mind that he was being told the truth.

The passage through that tunnel of Sapperton, which, on a sudden bend of the canal, opens a deep black mouth into the heart of the hills, was the only time when the voyage of the *Flower of Gloster* had in it the sense of stirring adventure. Into the grim darkness you glide and, within half an hour, are lost in a lightless cavern where the drip drip of the clammy water sounds incessantly in your ears.

Some time ago, when there was more constant traffic on this canal, there were professional leggers to carry you through ; for there is no tow-path, and the barge must be propelled by the feet upon the side walls of the tunnel. Now that the barges pass so seldom, this profession has become obsolete. There are no leggers now. For four hours Eynsham Harry and I lay upon our sides on the wings that are fitted to the boat for that purpose, and legged every inch of the two and three-quarter miles. It is no gentle job. Countless were the number of times I looked on ahead to that faint pin-point of light ; but by such infinite degrees did it grow larger as we neared the end, that I thought we should never reach it.

"What used the leggers to be paid ?" I asked after the first mile, when it seemed all sensation had gone out of my limbs and they were working merely in obedience to the despairing effort of my will.

"Five shillings, sir, for a loaded boat. Two and six for an empty one."

I groaned.

"A pound wouldn't satisfy me," said I.

"No, sur, I suspects not. It's always easier to do these things for nothing."

For an hour that was all we said. For an hour I legged away, thinking how true that casual statement was—"It's always easier to do these things for nothing." It is—always. All labour would be play were it not for payment. The man who reckons is worse than lost, he is made ; than which there can be no more bitter a punishment. Once, then, the labourer is paid, he begins a-reckoning of his hire, and that is all. From this come revolution and anarchy.

But one does not think of this sort of thing for long while legging it through Sapperton Tunnel. A drip of shiny water on one's face is quite enough to upset the most engrossing contemplation. I saw the pin-point of light growing to the pin's head, and still we laboured on, only resting a few moments to light a fresh piece of candle or take breath.

It was evening when we came out into the light again and, though the sun had set, with shadows falling everywhere, it almost dazzled me. A barge in the next lock rose above the lock's arms, with every line cut out against the pale sky.

XXXIX

HARD-BOILED EGGS

THE sense that an adventure is drawing towards its close makes the future look somewhat desolate and uninteresting. After Sapperton and the Golden Valley I felt as if the end had come already, though there were many miles of water to traverse before we reached the last lock at Inglesham.

I was harking back over the last three weeks, the amazing sunlight in it all, the glorious country ; sitting, I have no doubt, in an attitude somewhat disconsolate. We were passing under the bridge at Latton, where the road runs over the canal and frames with its arch an orchard where the butter-cups throw back the sunshine into the apple trees.

"You be very thoughtsome, sur," said Eynsham Harry presently, whereby I made certain he had been watching me.

"I'm thinking," said I, "that in a few days I shall be back again in London, and the band will be playing Gilbert and Sullivan in Charing Cross Gardens. There will be a roar of traffic from the Strand, and a dull incessant thunder of the trams along the Embankment. By eight o'clock the whole night will be full of light signs. Lipton's tea, Dewar's whisky, and Californian wines will be blaspheming the sky. Paper-boys will come shouting past my windows of murders I'd far sooner not know about. There may be a piano thumping its notes discordantly against the music of the band. I shall see the people through the windows of the Hotel Cecil feeding themselves, and waiters running here, there, and everywhere with plates. That's what I'm thinking about. It's enough to make you think, when your holiday is over. And talking about feeding, what have we got for lunch?"

Eynsham Harry shook his head.

"There's still a piece of that tongue, sur, and I can do wi' bread and cheese myself."

But that was not what I wanted at all. I thought of the chandler's shop where I often get my eggs, of the ham-bone which lies on a plate in the window and for ever seems to be in the last stages of boniness. I should soon be eating those eggs for breakfast again, and wanted, for the last time, perhaps, till next summer, to taste an egg with all its country freshness.

" I want some eggs," said I.

" There's no place, sur," said he, " nearer than Marston Meysey where you might get 'en."

" And how far's that ? "

" Well, sur, you come along the canal here two

miles and get out there at a bridge.   'Tis then two miles by the road."

" I'd walk more than that," said I.

" Then Marston Meysey's your place," he replied ; and to the village of Marston Meysey, when we had come to the bridge he spoke of, I started off to get my last meal of country eggs.

It is a winding, twisted road to this little village,

with high hedges at either side.   Most of the way
it was more lane than road.   At every turning some
other lane led out of it, till I had almost lost my way,
and began to despair of ever reaching this Marston
Meysey where I was to find my country eggs.   Two
young women driving in a farmer's trap over a
narrow bridge that spanned a stream came to my
rescue.

"Turn," said they, "to the right where 'ee see
the barn, then go on for half a mile; but don't turn to
the left.   Turn to the right again, and follow the
lodigraph wires.   'Twill take 'ee straight into the
village."

"Have you just come from there?" I asked.

They nodded their heads, and the flaps of their
linen bonnets nodded with them.

"Well, can you," said I, "tell me where it's
possible to get some new-laid eggs?"

"They be sold at t'bakers.   'Tis on the right of
street as 'ee go into the village."

I found it right enough then, one of those country
villages in England "the world forgetting, by the
world forgot."   It must be miles from anywhere;
far from the main road, a miniature colony of people
contained within themselves.

The baker's was not a shop: just a bake-house,
which was a part of an old building standing some
twenty odd yards off the village street.   In the cobbled
yard before it was an old leaden pump, and, with a
drip of water falling close to his nose, an old dog lay

beneath the spout contentedly asleep until I entered the five-barred gateway into the yard. Immediately he heard the creak of the hinges, he was on his legs and threatening me with a thousand imprecations if I came a step closer.

"Poor old feller," said I.

He knew that sort of cajoling, and would have none of it.

"You're a cross old fellow, aren't you?" I went on persuasively.

He said that that had nothing to do with it. I had no right in that yard. And I have no doubt the argument would have gone on without my getting a step nearer, had not a girl come out of the house, telling him just what she thought of him and where, if he were worth anything as a dog, he would be lying at that moment. After that he walked sulkily away, muttering under his breath words to the effect that she did not know human nature as well as he did.

"You'd let anybody in," said he.

"Go and lie down," said she.

"That's all you can say," he muttered.

"Go and lie down," she repeated, and she stamped her foot.

"Don't think much of that for an argument," he growled, and he tumbled into his barrel, resting his face between his paws, never taking his eyes off me. Even then, he could not keep quite silent, but continued to mumble in a deep note under his breath the

word "Thief." If you say it in a guttural way
yourself, you can just imagine the sound of it.

"He doesn't like strangers," said the little girl.

"Whereas you trust everybody," said I.

"It depends what they look like," she replied.

It was as good as asking me to speak of myself,
and as no man refuses such invitation when it is
proffered him, I asked her if she meant that she
passed me as trustworthy. She eyed me shyly,
making me remember that I had not been in the
company of her sex for one whole month.

"Well?" said I—and as I said it, I felt my eye
meet hers. Now whether there was that in my expression which conveyed my thoughts to her intuition,
I would not swear, but she blushed. Then she looked
charming, and her eyes dropped. At that moment
the dog said "Thief" again.

"Shall we leave it at that?" said I.

"At what?"

"At what the dog said."

"I didn't hear him," said she.

"Perhaps it's as well," said I. "Now hadn't I
better tell you what I want?"

She nodded her head and, because she thought we
were about to begin business, raised her eyes again.
Accordingly I talked business steadily—the business
about the eggs—for five minutes. The woman who
has said she will never speak to you again is always
amenable to conversation if you talk business. You
may mean what you like—in fact, the more you

mean, the more ready is she to talk. Whenever I stopped and she found me watching her, she would say no more. So I asked that the eggs might be boiled then and there.

"I want them for lunch," said I, "and have got no place to boil them in."

"I thought you said you were on a barge," she replied. "Haven't you got a stove in the cabin?"

"Thief!" said the dog in the barrel.

"That's quite true," I answered, and I took no notice of the dog. "We have a stove and a saucepan and an egg-timer. I told the lie in order to stop a little longer and talk to you."

Now when you tell a lie to a woman and she knows it is a lie, she is so amazed when you admit it that she takes it as a compliment. A barefaced truth only insults her. What is more, the admission of the lie will often make her laugh. And that is a mood when a woman will forgive you anything.

The little girl took the four brown eggs without a word, put them in a saucepan with some water and placed them on a fire which was already burning in a little niche in the wall. She just added a stick or two, pouring a few drops of paraffin over it to make the whole blaze up.

" I want them hard," said I.

" You shall have them hard," said she.

For a while then, we stood together and watched the water boil. Once I looked out of the corner of my eyes at her face to find her staring down into the saucepan, her whole expression full of contemplation.

" A penny," said I suddenly.

She started.

" One penny," I repeated.

" Not for twenty pence," said she.

" Which means," said I with that intuitive egotism of my sex, " that you're thinking about me."

" Do you think a thought about you would be worth twenty pence ? " she asked.

" Thief ! " said the dog in the barrel.

"Not to speak," said I, and I ignored the dog again. " It 'ud be worth more than twenty pence to conceal."

She bent down and looked into the saucepan.

" It's boiling," said she.

" So am I," said I, " with curiosity."

" How are you going to take the eggs ? " she asked—" in your pocket ! "

" I'll take them," said I, " as you give them to me, in my hand."

" Then I'll put them in a bag," said she.

And so she did when they were boiled. With her little hand wrinkled already with hard work, she held out the bag by one corner and I took it by the other.

" And now," said I, " how much? " but somehow I hated asking it.

" Two pence," she replied. I don't think she minded in the least. It is only men who are sentimentalists over these matters. They have no head for business when they have a heart to count the coin.

" But two pence ! " I exclaimed. " There were four—four eggs."

" Halfpenny each," she replied.

" But the boiling ? "

" I won't charge you for that," said she.

" You can charge me anything you like for the boiling," said I, stooping to bribery, as is the habit of the best of us—" you can charge me anything you like if you'll tell me what you were thinking about just now."

" I won't charge you for the boiling," said she.

" Fool ! " said the dog in the barrel.

XL

DIETETICS

Eynsham Harry had begun his lunch when I returned.
A piece of cheese was balanced on a piece of bread,
and on its way to his mouth as I came over the
bridge.

"I've got four eggs," said I. "You must have
two."

"Bread and cheese be all I want, sur," he replied.
And it was all that he ate. It is surprising how
little they need, these men whose day is one of
strenuous labour from morning till evening. I
thought again of the diners and the waiters in
London, of the people who consume three and four
courses for lunch, six or seven for dinner and a few
hours later seat themselves down to supper—not with
an appetite, never with an appetite, but always with
the capacity to eat. I thought of the people themselves, men and women who, at the utmost, had
done three or four hours' work in the day—the
majority of them no work at all—men and women
who had never earned a meal in their lives ; some

234

of them who had not even made the money to pay
for it.

"Oh, you must have an egg," said I. "They
are already boiled."

He shook his head.

"Well, how on earth," I exclaimed, "do you
manage to live on so little? Sometimes you eat
an egg for breakfast, bread and cheese for lunch,
occasionally a piece of meat for dinner. There
are people in London who haven't done half your
work, eating meat five times a day and in twenty
different ways and dishes. Meat for breakfast,
lunch—even meat sandwiches at tea ; then dinner
and supper."

"How do they manage to get it down, sur?"

"I'm damned if I know," said I. "I suppose
much in the same way as you tramp ten miles
to find a bird's nest. It's part of their amusement.
They could no more walk ten miles than you could
eat what they do."

"Well, sur, then I be glad I be a-boating. I
suppose they'd make fun of my bread and cheese.
Oh, I be glad I be a-boating. It's good for the
stomach. Isn't there anyone to tell them how they
be upsetting their insides ? "

"There was a play written once," said I, "holding
them all up to ridicule. They went to see it in
hundreds and thousands, but everyone of them
thought how well it applied to his next-door neigh-

bour.   They knew of everyone whose vice was over-
eating—everyone but themselves."

"Well, that be strange, sur.   London's a 'mazing
city.   They say everything takes place there ; but
it seems to me that everything takes place outside,

and there they only talk about it.   Politics be only
talk.   The country's governed by the people who
work.   If a new measure's past, it's because men
have been working to make the need of it, and
they build great houses for folk who can say a lot
of words, so that they can talk about what's been
done, and not one of 'em knows the way to do it.
Do you see this old feller coming along here ? "

I looked and, under the bridge, drawing after him a light punt-shaped boat, came an old man with white hair and a soft hat that partially concealed it.

" Who is he ? " I asked.

" He keeps the hedges along the canal in order. Trims them up a bit so that the horses can pass by."

" But no barges do come along here, surely ? " said I. " We haven't seen one all the way from Sapperton."

" Don't say that to him, sur. He goes on working here day after day all year round, and every night he goes home he expects to find a letter from the Canal Company telling him he ain't wanted no longer. Don't tell him we haven't seen no barges, sur. He'll ask me first thing, and I shall tell him we see one at Kempsford, that place where the canal runs through the village with a high garden wall on one side and apple orchard on the other."

" That's the last place we came through," said I. " I remember it. But tell me, this old fellow gets the pension, doesn't he ? "

" He gets it—yes, sur ; but he don't spend it."

" Why not ? "

" He prefers working, sur, and this is the last job he'll have."

He had come up with us by this time, dragging his boat, now nearly filled with the cuttings of the hawthorn hedges, which no doubt he took home for burning.

" Good morning, gentlemen ! " said he.

"Good morning !" we replied.

"Have 'ee seen a barge coming down this way from Sapperton ?"

"One," Eynsham Harry replied : "went back from Kempsford yesterday morning."

His face brightened, and not only with pleasure, but with recognition. He remembered Eynsham Harry, and sat down on the side of the barge to talk with him. I looked at his face then. He had the clearest and the bluest eye I have ever seen. It might have belonged to a child, yet he was well over seventy.

"Will you have some food with us ?" said I.

"No, thank 'ee, sur. I've had my bit a good hour ago." He pointed to a red and white-spotted handkerchief that lay, wrapped about a bowl, in the bottom of his boat.

"Well, come now," he continued, taking no more heed of me, but addressing himself directly to Eynsham Harry, "'ee saw a boat. There hasn't been one down these ways, not so far as Inglesham, come the fourth o' last month. I don't know what they be going to do about this canal—there gets less water in her every day, and I keeps at it keeping down the hedges ; but you won't see a bit o' horse dung on the tow-path not between here and Inglesham."

"Well, as long as there's any traffic at all," I interrupted, "they won't close it up as long as you're alive."

"I should be glad to be sure of that, sur. I've

written two letters to the people at Gloucester, asking
'em if they thought they wouldn't require my services
any longer to let me know, so as I could get work elsewhere; but I gets no answer, only every week my little
bit of money. So I don't like to give the job up."

"No! You stick to it, Willum," said Eynsham
Harry, "a horse on the path is better'n two in the
stable. You stick to it."

He nodded his head, fully appreciating the advice.
We saw him later, when he had gone away, stopping
at a hawthorn bush which overhung the path. He
was lopping off the protruding branches and throw-
ing them into his boat.

XLI

THE LAST LOCK

The same evening we arrived at Inglesham, where the canal opens wide into a broad basin, across the still water of which the reflections of the high poplars fall with every quivering leaf faithfully traced again.

Along this last pound, between Dudgrove Lock and Inglesham, we passed without saying a word. Most of the time, in fact, Eynsham Harry walked on ahead with Fanny on the tow-path, leaving me to take my last hand at the tiller. It is an occupation to which you get so accustomed that it becomes as mechanical as the mere exercise of walking along the path. Nothing short of complete aberration would lead you to swing the tiller wrong. I have seen a woman steering while at the same time she prepared a meal and nursed a baby. Every now and again she would disappear into the cabin to fetch some dish or other, but never did she steer into the bank or meet the awkward corners beneath some bridge. Steering had become as much a mechanical

matter as that with me.   I scarcely knew the tiller
was in my hands.

At last, as we entered the basin by Inglesham
lock, I saw Eynsham Harry lay a hand on the tow-

line. Fanny stopped at once, and the rope sagged loose into the water.

"Here's the end of my journey," said I to myself, and I stepped down into the cabin to get my knapsack, which was already packed. When I came up again, Eynsham Harry was aboard up forard.

"This be Inglesham, sur," said he.

I nodded my head, and strapped my knapsack to my shoulder. Then we entered into arrangements about his taking the *Flower of Gloster* back to Coventry, where it was to be delivered in good order to Mr Phipkin, after which we strolled to the lock-head and stood there for a while looking down into the deep basin. Even there the poplars found their reflection. Indeed, they are truly princesses, always standing before some pool to gaze at their own faces.

"Well," I said at last, "this is the end of it. Here we part company," and I held out my hand. He shook it in a mighty grip.

"If ever you be wanting, sur," said he, "to come a-boating again, just write to me at the lock-house at Hillmorton, outside Rugby, and I'll take 'ee out as long a trip as 'ee likes on the *Henrietta*. That's my boat —called after my wife."

INGLESHAM
LOCK

"I'll work my way," said I, "if I'm competent."

"Oh, you be competent, sur, so be you get up early enough of a morning."

"I shall suit my ways to yours," said I, "even when it comes to a matter of birds'-nesting."

Then he held out his hand, and we shook again, after which I turned on my heel and set off across the meadows for the town of Lechlade.   Once I looked back.   He had turned the barge round in Inglesham Basin ; Fanny was hitched again to the tow-line, and the *Flower of Gloster* was on her homeward journey through those water-roads of England, back to her town of Coventry once more.